From Shtetl to Suburbia
The Family in Jewish Literary Imagination

From Shtetl to Suburbia

The Family in Jewish Literary Imagination

Sol Gittleman

Illustration by Steven Trefonides

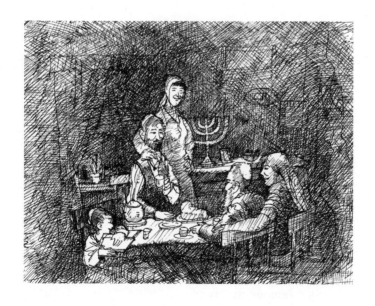

BEACON PRESS   Boston

i

Beacon Press books are published under the auspices
of the Unitarian Universalist Association
Published simultaneously in Canada by
Fitzhenry & Whiteside Limited, Toronto
Printed in the United States of America

(hardcover) 9 8 7 6 5 4 3 2 1

Library of Congress Cataloging in Publication Data

Gittleman, Sol, 1934–
    From shtetl to suburbia.
    Bibliography: p. 177
    Includes index.
    1. Yiddish literature—History and criticism.
    2. American literature—Jewish authors—History
    and criticism. 3. Jews in literature. I. Title.
PJ5120.G5   839'.09   78-53646
ISBN 0–8070–6364–9

To Julia, Peter and Thomas

Contents

Contents

From Shtetl to Suburbia:
The Family in Jewish Literary Imagination

Prologue

The focus of this study is quite clear and specific. We wish to examine the phenomenon of Yiddish literature as it emerged out of the disintegration of East European life in Czarist Russia after 1881; and then to trace the migration of that literature to the United States, both in its Yiddish and American forms. We are concerned with a relatively brief period of history—less than a century.

Yet in order to understand the forces which brought about the extraordinary birth of what has become a major literature in the Western tradition, we have to retrace the adventurous past of both the peoples involved, namely the Jews of Russia and Poland, and their language, Yiddish, which is so intimately tied up with the flowering of that literature. The Jewish dilemma in Czarist Russia, the availability of a language which until that moment was looked upon with mocking condescension even by those who spoke it, the concentration of millions of Jews in tiny towns, *shtetls* as they were called, and finally the assassination of one Czar, Alexander II, and the assumption of power by another, Alexander III: these were the immediate events which caused the sudden metamorphosis of what had been a most dubious literary instrument. But to fully understand these events we must go back even further, to the roots of the Yiddish language, to the early history of the Jewish presence in Europe. For the literature that ultimately emerged is very much a product of two thousand years of Jewish history since the exile from Palestine, and even more so a byproduct of a language which until the late nineteenth century was looked upon as the homeliest, most miserable means of expression, clearly unfit for serious intellectual activity. To understand the meaning of *Yiddishkeit*, the cultural value system of the Jewish *shtetl*, we have to explore the cultural and linguistic wanderings which ulti-

1

mately led the Jew to this decisive moment in his history. Only then can we fully comprehend the nature of the Yiddish world of East European Jewry before the Holocaust, and how that world has managed to survive even when the means of its expression, the Yiddish language, has nearly ceased to exist.

For there was another reason why this cultural heritage has survived, in spite of every reasonable argument that it should not have. *Yiddishkeit,* more than anything else, has come to mean *mishpoche,* the idea of "family," of kinship, of being a part. At a time when the Jewish identity seemed to be challenged by all the forces of modernity during the past century, it was only natural that the writers who spoke to the world of the Jewish masses should focus on the threat to the family. Later, when the center of the Yiddish-speaking world had shifted to America, the preoccupation with family identity, with the threat of assimilation, remained just as strong; finally, when the Yiddish language had disappeared altogether, when the bonds of Jewishness had completely come apart, it was the English-speaking Jewish-American writers who once again turned to the themes of kinship to remind the Jew in America who he was and what the price of this assimilation would be.

Introduction

The Hebrew word *mishpoche* has found its way into every language spoken by Jews for the past two thousand years. Whether in Palestine or in African or European exile, this word for family has come to express the deepest sense of relationship that Jew can have to Jew. Its meaning transcends its application to merely narrow familial associations. There is a saying, "all Jews are *mishpoche*," and in this we see the intense feeling of common heritage, common obligations, and common values which often set apart historically persecuted minorities—Gypsies, Armenians, and Jews, for example—from their tormentors.[1]

But during the last century events have occurred which have so profoundly shaken the foundations of Jewish life that the concept of *mishpoche* has taken on an even more desperate connotation, one that goes to the heart of the question of existence for the Jews. Beginning with the breakdown of the Yiddish-speaking, East European world of the wretched Jewish townlet, the *shtetl* of Czarist Russia and Poland, the assault on Jewish identity has been traumatic, particularly in terms of the continued presence of the *mishpoche*, both in the narrow and the wider meanings of the word. The East European world had survived nearly five centuries of persecution and the threat of extinction. It had grown strong in its traditions of loyalty, of family, and of belonging to the God of Israel. This was the world of *Yiddishkeit*, totally identified with a language beloved by the masses and hated by the Jewish intellectuals: Yiddish. It was the struggle over language which helped precipitate the intrusion of the outside world into these sleepy Jewish towns toward the end of the nineteenth century. Deeply religious, millions of *shtetl* Jews were followers of the great Hassidic rabbis who preached a simple message of joy, faith, and tradition.

But the modern age was tearing at the fabric of Jewish life. Socialism, Zionism, even more virulent anti-Semitism finally broke through and penetrated the experience of these people. Out of the turmoil, Yiddish literature emerged as the vehicle for communication, and it focused on the theme which was central to Jewish identity: the *mishpoche,* the family, caught up in a time of change.

Eventually, the struggle led to the end of this traditional world. Some remained behind and waited for the Russian Revolution, but millions left Czarist Russia to produce one of the greatest people's migrations ever recorded. By the outbreak of World War I, nearly two million Jews had settled in New York City alone, and a new sense of both crisis and identity as a Jew swept over the *mishpoche.* With the death of six million Jews in Europe, the American Jew faced a challenge to survival which even surpassed the grimness of the death camps in its threat to Jewish existence: assimilation and the easy freedom of life in America. Again, the response of Jewish literature, this time not in Yiddish but in English, concentrated on the theme of the Jewish family as the key to Jewish identity.

This is the scope of the present study. It pivots around two worlds: one in Eastern Europe, flavored by centuries of traditions, steeped in a familiar language of associations, oppressed but also comfortable, insofar as one could survive with one's customs intact and a grudging acceptance of perpetual oppression. Then, there occur the events which suddenly and dramatically overwhelm that world, which alter it completely. The second pole is in America, where the Jew has found all the freedom and opportunity which he never experienced in the *shtetl.* But he has had to pay a price, the price of his identity. Besides looking at the imaginative literary expression which is associated with these two worlds, this book will also attempt to place the historical and cultural evolution into some context.

4

The thread which runs through both of these worlds, however, is the Jewish preoccupation with kinship, with family, with *mishpoche*. Whether in Yiddish or in English, in the *shtetl* or suburbia, the Jew has always accepted the threat to his survival, and his response has always been in terms of the bonds of Jewishness.

1
The Roots and Growth of Yiddish

THE Jews have had many languages in the five thousand years of their existence. Yiddish has been only one of them, and the literary traditions in that language have lasted scarcely more than a century, from mid-nineteenth to mid-twentieth. As a living, spoken language, its history goes back to the thirteenth century, perhaps, but it is unlikely that it will survive much beyond the twentieth. Furthermore, the Yiddish language seems really quite narrow, even sectarian, written in the cryptic Hebrew script, from right to left on the printed page, available and accessible only to those Jews who held on to what many called the language of the Ghetto. Yet the impact of this language, the culture associated with it, and the values which were translatable into other cultures have been enormous. Even where the original Yiddish is dying—in the Soviet Union, Israel, the United States, and South America—we find in Russian, Hebrew, English, and Spanish a continuation of the literary and cultural traditions associated with the world of Yiddish and the value system associated with it, which has been described as *Yiddishkeit*.

What is Yiddish? Where did it come from? Do all Jews speak it? In order to deal with these and other questions of culture and language, we have to chart the linguistic migrations of the Jewish people from the beginnings of the Diaspora (itself a Greek word). Up to that point, the "Jewish" languages described the role of Palestine in the Middle East. Basic was the Semitic language, Hebrew, the language of the Jewish Bible; and a more modern form, Aramaic, which was also used in parts of the Old Testament and the Talmudic writings. But the Jews of the Holy Land had been exposed to Greek and, beginning the pattern of linguistic assimilation which was to be repeated dozens of times in nations all over the world, the Jews took up the new language. The Hellenization of the Jewish world was considerable, and its effect on the spoken and written languages of the Jews strong. During the Roman occupation, Latin had some impact, but not nearly as great as Greek. In any case, when the Jews were finally driven out of Palestine after the Roman victory in 70 A.D., they took with them their Semitic languages, some Greek, and some Arabic dialects. The greatest movement was westward, across the face of North Africa. This is the point at which the Jewish people began their life-and-death struggle and started developing the sense of ethnic identity that has characterized them for centuries. The pivot was always language, and the threat was inevitably assimilation. The rabbis made a great effort to maintain a linguistic identity for the Jews, holding onto traditional Hebrew grammar, to Aramaic and the languages of the now inaccessible homeland. In order to trade commercially and to survive, the Jews picked up the local languages wherever they were and, when possible, adapted them to their own peculiar needs. One of these apparent eccentricities was the inevitable custom of writing the local language in Hebrew script, always from right to left, so that the Jew would never forget his basic Hebrew letters.

This practice continued throughout the period of post-exile Jewish wanderings across Africa, from the first to the eighth centuries of the Christian era. Jewish settlements could be found from Marrakech to Alexandria, but a significant number of Jews followed the invading armies of Tarik, an Arab chieftain, who in 711 A.D. crossed the Straits of Gibraltar and began the Moorish conquest of Spain.

The presence of significant numbers of Jews in Spain produced still another major linguistic challenge, this time a two-fold one. With the Muslim expansion in the eighth century, Arab culture flourished in the new Spanish environment. For the next four hundred years, Spanish and Arab armies fought over land in which the Jew had found relative security and stability. In return for this stability, the Jews exchanged part of their cultural habits. Within two generations after their arrival early in the eighth century in the wake of their Arab masters, more Jews were writing in adapted Spanish and Arabic languages than were communicating in the traditional Semitic tongues. Of course the specific peculiarities of Jewish writing were maintained: Hebrew letters were used, and the writing still went from right to left. The Judaeo-Spanish language of the Jews—called at times *Ladino* or *Judezmo*—became the vehicle for the first great European flowering of Jewish literature. The Spanish Jews, the *Sephardim*,[1] created a folk literature rich in imagery and style.

But of greater importance than the indigenous literature was the impact of Arabic on Jewish culture, particularly on Jewish scholarship. For all intents and purposes, the Spanish Jews exchanged Hebrew for Arabic as a means of serious learned discourse. The most notable scholar produced by the Jewish Renaissance in Spain was Moses Maimonides (1135–1204), who regularly wrote in Arabic, though still, of course, using the Hebrew alphabet. Even those writers who continued to express themselves in Hebrew were affected by the new languages of the Jews. Hebrew poetry of this period was particularly influenced by the style, imagery, form, and meter of Arab verse.

The serious, even deadly nature of the threat of assimilation did not occur until the eleventh century, when the Christian reconquest of Spain began in earnest. By the year 1200, Jews living under Christian rule had experienced the worst aspects of persecution. Some Jews had taken the easy road of conversion, a convenient alternative, particularly when it was taken with no purpose other than survival. Few of the Jewish converts took their Catholicism seriously, and these *conversos* were looked upon with some suspicion by the authorities. In 1391, these crypto-Jews were branded as *marranos,* swine, and were the victims of anti-Jewish riots throughout Spain. Therefore, in order to make their apparent conversion seem authentic, many Jews concentrated on the Spanish language and it became the everyday language of thousands of *converso* families. Indeed, it is the Spanish language which dominates the specific nature of Sephardic tradition, separates it from the non-Sephardic, and still gives Spanish-speaking Jewry today its unique characteristics. Even after the final expulsion of Jews from Spain in 1492, the Spanish language tradition of the Jews did not die. The Spanish Jews fled either to North Africa or to Turkey, where another rich Sephardic literary tradition continued, creating a vast number of Judaeo-Turkic languages based on Sephardic. Others found refuge in the Spanish colonies of the Lowlands, and, in Amsterdam in the sixteenth and seventeenth centuries, one of Europe's great Jewish literary and scholarly traditions flourished in the Sephardic *Ladino* as well as in the newly acquired Dutch language. In spite of that, a child of a Portuguese *marrano* family, Baruch Spinoza (1632–1677), caused a great outcry because it was considered a heresy for a Jew to write philosophical tracts in Latin. In 1656 Spinoza was excommunicated by the Amsterdam Sephardic community.

As early as the ninth century, many Jews from the Iberian peninsula had been welcomed by their brethren already living in France, and the refugees found fully established Jewish communities waiting for them. The most famous of French-

Jewish academies had been established at Troyes, where one of the great Jewish medieval scholars, Solomon ben Isaac (1040–1105), had written his important commentaries on the Bible. Rashi, as he was affectionately known by his followers, had established an academy in his native town. He was born and died a Frenchman, and his biblical commentaries sometimes give one the impression that he was more at home in his native French than he was in Hebrew. In his *marginalia,* Rashi would often translate difficult words into Judaeo-French, i.e., Old French, written once again in the Hebrew alphabet and from right to left. This language, known as *Laaz,* was the common means of discourse and commerce for the French Jews. Rashi's commentaries contain nearly ten thousand Old French words. In addition, we have other documents of Rashi's, primarily commercial transactions. He made his living as a wine merchant, and he had business dealings with both Jew and Gentile. His everyday language of communication with these fellow merchants was French. With the Gentiles, he wrote in the Roman script; with the Jews, he used the Hebrew. In both cases, the actual language was the same.

What is of particular significance is the overall degree of linguistic adaptation. The Jews, after a century of significant presence in France, had readily adapted to the native language. In Spain, in spite of the hazards of living in the midst of two religions warring with one another, the Jews had quickly taken to the languages of both factions. The Jew, inevitably, seemed ready for linguistic assimilation. And Germany now offered an even greater opportunity.

The Emergence of Yiddish

The Jews began settling in considerable numbers in the Rhineland as early as the tenth century. Soon thereafter they had established major academic centers for Talmudic study at Worms, Speyer, and Mainz. The history of the Jew in Western Europe before the Crusades was not one marked by particular religious hostility. The Jews as traders, as artisans, and as simple townsfolk, were looked upon with the same attitude as Greek, Syrian or Phoenician traders; they were somewhat exotic, understood trade and commerce, and had connections with their fellow Jews around the world. In religious affairs, the Jew even had a special place: all other non-Christian religions had been officially banned, but not the religion of the Jews. Thus, when the Jew came to the German-speaking lands, he received the same welcome he had been given elsewhere in Europe. Once again, the same linguistic "hospitality" became evident. Within two generations, the Jews of the Rhineland had quite easily taken to the native Rhenish dialect of Middle High German. There was sufficient commercial and social intercourse to permit the Jewish community ready access to both the culture and the language of the German natives. Not only did the Jews take the Germans' language, they also took their myths. By 1200, the Rhineland Jews spoke and wrote *Ivri-Teutsch, Judenteutsch,* or *Jüdisch,* as this language was variously described. Again, with remarkable consistency, the language was written from right to left in the Hebrew alphabet. But most astonishing, the oldest written documents we have in this new language of the German Jews are adaptations of German folk sagas and love poems. The oldest extant version of the German *Gudrun* saga is in *Jüdisch,* and there is also a fourteenth-century Judaeo-German *Nibelungenlied.* There was even a Jewish troubadour-poet, Süsskind von Trimberg, who was a contemporary of the great German Minnesingers.

The Jews themselves soon identified their newly acquired language as *Yiddish,* or German spoken by Jews. Its dominance of Jewish life outside the synagogue was total. It became almost immediately the exclusive means of communication in trade and daily discourse. Of course, Hebrew remained, for the scholars, the Holy Tongue, the *loshen ha-*

12

kodesh, the only language suitable for liturgical practices. However, Yiddish became the mother tongue, the *mama-loshen,* the Jews' everyday garment. Its use quickly spread throughout Western Europe.

But something was happening in the political and social climate which was to affect the demography of Yiddish as a language and means of expression from that time on. The end of the eleventh century brought forth the phenomenon of the Crusades, which meant a totally new image for the Jew in Europe, a new, unfortunate role which was to replace the earlier one marked by a more or less benevolent acceptance. The church militant emerged as a force bent on either the conversion of the Jews or their destruction. The Jew as pariah, as an outcast not fit to associate with Christians, became a stereotype which established itself at the same time the Jewish community in Germany totally embraced its new language of Yiddish as the primary means of discourse. By the time of the Fourth Lateran Council of 1215, the Jew was recognized as an alien. The concept of the ghetto was accepted as the proper mode of having Jews live among Gentiles, and the former spirit of mutual trust and acceptance gave way to a hostility which left its mark on both groups. This was a period of violent pogroms against Jewish communities all over Europe. For their part, the Jews accepted the concept of the ghetto as perhaps the only means of protection; they grew to prefer their own people as neighbors; they shunned the social and cultural worlds which formerly welcomed them.

They had at least a means of communication by this time, and even a language which could, in its written form, assist them in protecting themselves. Yiddish, as a spoken and written language, had become a *lingua franca* even among Sephardic Jews, who were required to know some Yiddish for business purposes. Even when Jewish women could not read or write Hebrew—which was often the case—they could communicate in Yiddish, which literally every Jew in Western Europe, even the Sephardim, could at least read. In its written form, with its Hebrew alphabet, it was almost impenetrable to non-Jews, very few of whom had mastered the Jewish written forms.

Even more important for the future of the European Jews and their language, after 1215 a policy of forced expulsion was adopted throughout the German lands. Jews were banished with increasing frequency from the land which they had for several centuries identified as their home. At the same time, coincidentally, Polish princes far to the east, eager to establish some commercial system of their own which might give them parity with the advanced economic systems in Western Europe, invited some Jewish entrepreneurs to settle in Poland. When the word got out that Jews were welcomed in the East, there began a wholesale migration of thousands of Rhenish Jews, a movement which lasted for fully a century, and which shifted the center of Yiddish linguistic activities. By 1500, Yiddish had spread even further and was the common language of European Jewry from the Vistula to the British Isles.[2]

The Earliest Forms of Yiddish Literature

Although the majority of Jews had already begun to leave Germany by the mid-thirteenth century in the hope of finding sanctuary in the East, many remained in western ghettoes and they are the ones who continued both the literary and linguistic traditions which had grown up around the new Yiddish language, even during and after the persecutions and massacres. It was these people, writing and speaking Yiddish in Western Europe, who have provided the majority of Yiddish literary documents from that earliest period until the Enlightenment.

In spite of the brutalities inflicted on them during the bloody thirteenth and fourteenth centuries, Jews remained fascinated by the medieval romances of the Gentile world. Jewish versions of legends like those of King Arthur or Theodoric (Dietrich von Bern), thoroughly "de-Christian-ized," circulated freely. The most imaginative of these Yid-dish adaptations of bardic material was the *Shmuel Bukh* (The Book of Samuel), an epic retelling of the story of Samuel, the reign of King Saul, and concluding with the story of David. Written sometime during the mid-fifteenth century, the poem is in the classical German epic stanza form; David, the Jewish king, takes on all the noble, chivalric character-istics of a Siegfried.

The most popular of these Yiddish works of chivalry was the product of the first identifiable Yiddish writer of stature, Elijah Levita (1469–1549), a Nuremberg-born humanist who spent the greater part of his life in Italy. There he became interested in Anglo-French romances, and in 1507 he trans-lated *Bovo d'Antona,* an Italian version of the Bevis of Hampton tales, into Yiddish. It soon was known as the *Bove-Bukh* and represents the first example of Renaissance *ottava rima* in Yiddish. Levita's stories in Yiddish circulated through-out Western Europe as *bove-mayses (mayse* meaning tales in Hebrew). *Bove* was soon confused with *Bobe,* the Yiddish word for grandmother; this resulted in the phrase *Bobe-mayse,* or grandmother's tale, which came to mean an in-credible tale of imagination and romance.

A Literature for Women

One of the early editions of the *Bove-Bukh* carried on the title page: "For all pious women"; and indeed, from the out-set Yiddish had a remarkable relationship with its female audience, a relationship which ultimately was to affect the development of the language as a literary instrument. Yiddish developed into a means of expression which served the special needs of Jewish women in what would have to be identified as a male chauvinist Jewish world. Even though the Jewish woman enjoyed enormous advantages over her Gentile counterpart, she was still far from free to study Talmudic tracts or Torah to her satisfaction. Traditionally, Hebrew had not been the language for women. It was the holy tongue, the language of study, of Scripture, and as such reserved for males. At best, Jewish women had a smattering of Jewish learning; there was never any question of equal educational opportunity in the Jewish medieval world, although we do have occasional records of females attending Yeshivas. Yiddish, then, was a common language that provided the means for both study and entertainment for Jewish women all over Europe. Almost from the beginning of its use as a literary language, Yiddish was intended quite specifically for a female audience. The romances formed one major segment of these writings; the other segment was religious or ethical in nature. Parables, homilies, biblical stories, parts of the Old Testament, parts of the various commentaries on the Bible, the Psalms, all found their way into Yiddish, with prefaces, specifically addressed to the female reader, on how to elevate one's mind. The most comprehensive of these anthologies was the *Mayse Bukh,* a collection of 257 stories published in Basel in 1602. It contains chivalric tales mixed in with miracle stories of wonder rabbis, Maimonides, Rashi, and others. This edition opens with a statement to "ye dear dames," in which the anonymous collector admits that he hopes to provide edification and entertainment.

The most important of all these Yiddish books for women is the *Ze'enah u-Re'enah* (a Hebrew phrase taken from the *Song of Songs* and pronounced *Tsenerene* in Yiddish), written around 1590 by Jacob Ashkenazi. The Hebrew phrase of the title means "Come and See," which is exactly what the author intended to suggest to his readers. The main body consists of Yiddish discourses and translations from the Pentateuch, parts of the Prophets, as well as the Book of Esther, with generous comments and moral admonitions. All in all, it was a simplified volume of Jewish learning in a language known to a segment of the population which otherwise would not have had access to it. For the Jewish women in search of some scholarly orientation, it was exactly what they wanted, short of the original material in Hebrew. This volume soon became the standard reading material for the Sabbath for Jewish women all over Europe. It has gone through more editions than any other work of Yiddish writing. It is still read by the same audience of Jewish women for whom Hebrew will always be a mystery.

We can see, then, that there was a certain sexist element in the development of Yiddish as a literary language. For all Ashkenazic Jews, Yiddish was most definitely the daily means of communication, for business transactions, even when dealing with the Sephardim, who primarily spoke or wrote Ladino. But when it came to learning or serious literature, for the male Ashkenazic Jew Hebrew was the only means of intellectual discourse, both in written and spoken form. The Holy Tongue was intended for higher, liturgical matters, for which Yiddish was simply not appropriate. We can now see the deeper meaning of the term mama-loshen: it meant, quite literally, "The tongue of the mothers," of the women.

This label stuck to Yiddish for centuries. For hundreds of years, Yiddish was looked upon as a linguistic stepchild, a "jargon" perfectly suited for everyday street talk, business, jokes, and women.[3] It would not be until the great flowering of Yiddish literature in the middle of the nineteenth century that the language would be recognized as a suitable means of serious discussion.

Yiddish: East and West

The Jews who migrated to the East took with them a newly discovered suspicion of the Gentile world. The horrors of the Crusades left the Jews with a stronger sense of alienation, and with the Lateran Council's establishment of the ghetto, the Jews no longer had the easy linguistic access that had permitted them for centuries to absorb the speech of their Gentile neighbors. Yiddish, the most recently acquired Jewish language, now was more thoroughly cut off from surrounding sources. Particularly in the East, there was relatively little contact with the Slavic languages of Poland and Russia. The history and development of Yiddish are complex, but at the simplest level we have a language which is approximately eighty percent Germanic in vocabulary, with perhaps eight percent Hebrew elements (religious words particularly), the remainder coming from Slavic, Romance, and other sources. The basic grammatical model follows the German language, with some syntax resembling the Slavic. But Yiddish has a grammar, a *bona fide* structure, with case, gender, and all the semantic motivation required of a full-fledged language; it is not jargon, and it never has been. The written system is, as in the case of almost all languages of the Jews until the eighteenth century, based on the Hebrew alphabet, with variations of orthography in vowel signs. In terms of demography, until the end of the eighteenth century Yiddish was the virtually uncontested medium of oral communication among Jews from the Atlantic Ocean to the Ukraine.

Yiddish had established itself in a variety of ways. After centuries of wandering across Africa and Europe, finding and losing languages, acquiring cultural baggage, the Jews had finally found a common means of communication, which still provided them with the kind of privacy and exclusivity that an oppressed minority needs. The Jews—like the Armenians and the Gypsies—had acquired a means of contact with one another that permitted them to maintain their self-imposed and outward-imposed isolation. Occasionally, others saw the advantage. No sooner had Yiddish emerged in the Middle Ages as a crypto-language for Jews than it was embraced by beggars, vagabonds, and thieves as their means of private communication as well. They picked up Yiddish from Jewish innkeepers on the roads, as well as from roving bands of Jewish desperadoes. The Germans call it *Gaunersprache*, the language of thieves. For centuries, police authorities were puzzled by the phenomenon of the German underworld's relationship to the Yiddish language. Underworld correspondence was conducted in written Yiddish, thereby providing a code language which the authorities could not decipher. It was not until the middle of the nineteenth century that the riddle was thoroughly explained, and then by the chief of police of Lübeck, Germany, a particularly scholarly law enforcement officer named Friedrich Christian Benedict Avé-Lallement, who wrote a four-volume study of the language of the German criminal world.[4] The result was the first thorough grammar of the Yiddish language produced in Germany, as well as a detailed vocabulary listing of all Yiddish words found in the German *Gaunersprache*, by region. For example, the word for prostitute in Hamburg, Germany, was *eine Mesuse*. A *mezuzah*, for observant Jews, is a portion of the Pentateuch, encased in a small box, and attached to the doorpost of a Jewish home. Traditionally, as a Jew passes the object, he touches it with his fingertips, which he then kisses. The extension to the activities of the streetwalker can be clearly seen. Similarly, words such as *ganef* (a crook), *shammes* (in German, a private detective; in Yiddish, the guardian of the synagogue), and *duchenen* (a priestly function in Yiddish; in German, to steal from beneath one's eyes) appear in both languages. By the time Avé-Lallement had finished his study, the fourth and final volume was by itself a German-Yiddish dictionary of underworld terminology.

So this earliest period in the development of Yiddish as a

language of the Jews comes to an end, but not without some important characteristics taking hold of the hearts and minds of Europe's Jews and the language they had developed. First of all, the language had the flavor of intimacy. The Jew wore his Yiddish the way he wore his everyday garment, his familiar weekday gabardine. The language took on all the domestic nuances of the ghetto, of religious life, of family ties. Particularly, it remained close to the Jew during the period of greatest danger during and immediately after the Crusades. Second, as we have seen, familiarity did breed contempt, particularly in terms of the relationship of Yiddish and the Jewish woman. It was not considered a language fit for male intellectual activity. Finally, it suffered from the additional anti-social stigma associated with its use by the criminal world. It was, for some Jewish intellectuals and learned men, the language of the *proste,* of the low-life, fit for use in making a living perhaps, but not a language to be taken seriously.

These attitudes were to play a major role in the dramatic course of events which was to find the development of the Yiddish language at the center of a revolution in Jewish life. In one part of this life, Yiddish was to flourish; in the other, it was destined to die.

2

The Revolutions of Heart
and Mind:
Hassidism and Haskalah

INITIALLY, the Jews who had accepted the invitation of the Polish princes in the thirteenth century found a warm reception in the East. King Boleslaw the Pious gave his personal protection to all synagogues, and full and equal rights were extended to Jew and Christian alike under this remarkable ruler. Casimir the Great (1333–70) continued these policies, and under his rule the concept of the Jewish town developed. Casimir permitted the Jews to rent entire villages, and the Jews, still suffering the memories of pogroms in the West, conceived of an enclave, a self-contained town in which they could feel protected from future threats. In this fashion, the Jewish community itself first conceived the *shtetl,* the Jewish communal town of Eastern Europe which was destined to develop into the major means of settlement, later involuntary, for the millions of Jews in Russia and Poland. But the period of mutual acceptance ended at the close of the fifteenth century, by which time Jews all over Europe were sharing a similar existence, one marked by poverty and wretchedness.

In the face of a situation which could have marked the end of Jewish religious life had the people equated their despair with their religious preference, the orthodox rabbinate held on tightly to the discipline of Talmudical rule, with its rigid, inflexible interpretations. After all, it had been the Talmud which had provided the Jews with a remarkably advanced body of knowledge during the first millennium in Europe, knowledge that permitted the Jews to provide feudal civilizations with the necessary rules of governance out of which commerce could develop. The Talmud dealt in very specific and cultivated terms with matters of contracts, transactions, torts, business and commercial activities. It also provided the ethical frame of reference which was required for these activities to work effectively. Now, with life harsh, the rabbis turned once more to their laws, in order to offer to the Jewish masses some system of survival in the face of potential extinction.

But something else was needed, some manifestation less rigid, more flexible, more hopeful. The Jewish masses found this in a body of literature which became known as the Kabbalah. Basically, Kaballah is a unique structure which sums up Jewish mysticism, and from its origins in thirteenth-century Spain to its temporary decline in the face of the eighteenth-century Enlightenment, it dominated the imagination of European Jewry.

Kabbalah is not one book, but if one book were wanted to characterize and to represent the essence of Kabbalistic thought, it would be the *Zohar* (*The Book of Splendor*), which appeared in Spain late in the thirteenth century. Kabbalah gave the Jews a heady draught of exaltation, emotion, a religion of ecstasy and mystery. It provided Judaism with a hidden meaning, with a way beyond the orthodoxy of rabbinical strictures. Above all, Kabbalah offered the downtrodden Jews a magical way to find God. Out of its unique teachings came the vast structure of cryptic formulae which made it so appealing to the Jewish masses. At heart it was messianic, and it gave every miserable Jew the opportunity to help bring about the coming of the Messiah. For each Jew had the chance to help solve the mystery, to find the right formula, symbol, sign which might speed up the arrival of the Savior. Taking the numerical values assigned to the Jewish alphabet, Jews all over the world would add up the total value of the five Books of Moses, divide by the number of times the word for God appears, and emerge with the date for the end of the world. At its best, Kabbalah stressed simple faith in God, a direct communication of the individual with the Supreme Being, who could reveal Himself to the most insignificant wretch on earth. At its worst, Kabbalah became an elaborate, often eccentric system of astrology, hocus-pocus, and even erotica.[1] But perhaps its greatest influence was felt when it helped usher in the Messianic Era, or rather False Messianic Era, which dominated Jewish thought from the middle of the seventeenth to the middle of the eighteenth centuries.

Indeed, the Kabbalistic writings were the only optimistic force that Jews in the Gentile Renaissance and Reformation period had to fall back on. There was little physical "rebirth" for European Jewry during the great age of Europe's Renaissance, and Luther's Reformation, after initially offering some hope of improvement, proved to be a bitter disappointment. Luther had wanted the Jews to support his efforts to overthrow Rome's hegemony, but when the Jews realized that Luther had mass conversion in mind, they politely but definitely rejected Lutheranism. At this the great reformer called them "the most stiff-necked of all of God's children," cursed them, and called them ingrates for turning away from God's will.

The Jews were fully caught up in the horrors of the Christian wars, particularly the Thirty Years' War (1618–48). In fact, the year 1648 was singled out by Kabbalists and mystics from Judaism, Catholicism, and Protestantism alike as a year to mark. The Jews were even more convinced of it when the Polish Cossacks under Bogdan Chmielnetski revolted that year against landowners and some Jewish tax collectors, a revolt that turned into a pogrom in which nearly one hundred thousand Jews were slaughtered—up to that time certainly Europe's worst pogrom. The Kabbalah provided an explana-

tion: the Messiah would come only after enormous Jewish suf-
ferings. The Chmielnetski massacres certainly seemed to be
the sign that the Messiah's arrival was imminent. Therefore,
when in 1648 the Jewish world was rocked by the appearance
of a particularly strong claimant to the role of Messiah, everyone, including the Gentile world, waited in anticipation. The
claimant was Shabbatai Zevi (1626–1676), born in Smyrna,
Turkey, trained in the Kabbalah, filled with a sense of super-
natural power, and the leader of a wildly enthusiastic group
of disciples. Zevi was immediately denounced by the rabbinical hierarchies all over Europe, but led his followers
through the Middle East. In Cairo, announcing that God his
Father had told him to marry one touched by evil, he cele-
brated his wedding to a Jewish prostitute who had had a
vision that she was to be the bride of the future Messiah. In
1665, he returned to his native Smyrna to announce that the
moment was at hand. Amid shouts of "The Messiah has
come!" Jews flocked to Zevi's side from all over Europe and
the Middle East, selling their property, abandoning their families, as they prepared for the trek to the Holy Land. Meanwhile, Zevi had established himself in the style of a Middle
Eastern potentate, living in splendor and very much filled
with his own sense of power. In 1666 he arrived in Constan-
tinople with a large group of followers, who called themselves Shabbataens. The sultan was more impressed with the
numbers than the claim of messiahship, and immediately had
Zevi arrested. He was given a choice: convert to the Moslem
faith, or be executed. The hopes of the Shabbataens were
shattered when their leader suddenly appeared in the Turk-
ish turban and announced his belief in Allah.

The dramatic rise and fall of the Shabbataen movement left
Jewish communities who had believed in it crushed and de-
moralized. Some diehards claimed that the conversion was
still part of the great plan, and the remnants are still active in

Turkey as members of a half-Jewish, half-Moslem religious group which follow the tenets of the Shabbataen code.

But Shabbatai Zevi's downfall only encouraged other false messiahs, and a wave of proclamations swept Europe. The most interesting was also the last of the serious pseudo-Messiahs, Jacob Frank (1726–1791). Frank took Kabbalah to its ultimate extreme. He announced that he was the heir of Shabbatai Zevi, whose spirit had come to Poland to find fulfillment. He informed the authorities that it was his intention to join all the churches of the world in a final unification, and that through sexual pleasure and gratification God would finally proclaim himself. Some of the Frankist ritual ceremonies turned into orgies, and church and rabbinic commissions were both suspicious of the heretical nature of this sect. In 1759, Frank and his fifteen thousand followers had themselves baptized as Catholics, and he settled down to a life of splendid opulence among his adherents in Germany.

Haskalah

By the mid-1800s, the situation for European Jewry was almost beyond despair, and nowhere was it worse than in Germany, or in those hundreds of small principalities, duchies, and dukedoms generally described as the German Lands. There had been no year of judgment, no coming of the Messiah. The Kabbalah had provided no solutions, the false Messiahs had left the people worse off than before, and with the exception of a handful of protected court Jews, so-called *Hofjuden* or *Schutzjuden*, the Jewish community was as wretched and impoverished as it had been hundreds of years earlier. The Messianic fervor had given way to strict rabbinical control once again. The sectarian parochialism of traditional orthodoxy came out of the Shabbataen and Frankist heresies strengthened. The German Jew, like his brethren throughout Europe, lived in squalid ghettoes, taxed beyond endurance, prohibited from walking among the Gentiles after dark, forced to wear the *Judenstern*, the Jewish star, on drab but peculiar clothing prescribed by law. The Jew was no better than the cattle of the fields, except that he did not have the freedom the animals had. The petty prince determined the size of the ghetto, who could have children, what work a Jew could do; in short, the Jew was a slave. No German prince was better than any other in this respect; not even Frederick the Great showed any particular kindness toward his Jewish subjects. His anti-Jewish laws were just as rigid and unenlightened as were those of any of his neighbors.

It was into this grim environment that Moses Mendelssohn (1729–86) stepped. Born in Dessau, he had exhausted all the opportunities for learning that his native town could provide by the time he was fourteen. He was an outstanding Talmudic scholar, a rabbi, but physically exhausted by his childhood ordeal. He stammered and had quite early developed a hump to add to his physical problems. Nevertheless, young Moses ben Mendel was determined that his fate was not going to be that of so many other bright Talmudic students. He left Dessau, followed his teacher to Berlin, and there began the enormous task he had set for himself: the emancipation of German Jewry. Moses from Dessau first Germanized his name, and having gained access to a few well-placed Jewish families, he commenced a program of study unlike any engaged in by any other Yeshiva student. Within a matter of a few years, young Mendelssohn had mastered the German language, a remarkable feat for a German Jew. At that time, in the middle of the eighteenth century, there were no more than a handful of German Jews who could read the Roman letters or who could engage even fitfully in written German. Mendelssohn's accomplishment is all the more startling when one realizes that soon after he had begun his studies in German he was competing—and winning—prizes in essay writing and philosophy.

The Berlin intellectuals were astonished. Who was this young, deformed Jew who wrote such elegant German? Even Frederick was somewhat impressed, although he certainly never expressed much interest in his native language; he much preferred French, and considered German a language for wagon drivers. Mendelssohn was introduced to court, began associating with the leading lights of the German *Aufklärung*, beginning a particularly warm association with Lessing, who then immortalized his friend in that ultimate dramatic expression of the German Age of Reason, *Nathan der Weise* (*Nathan the Wise*).

It was not enough for Mendelssohn, however, to be welcomed at the German court. His major preoccupation was still with his fellow Jews, and all the intervention and good offices which he might be able to bring to bear would not accomplish his goal: the destruction of the ghetto. For that, Mendelssohn saw another means: the destruction of the Yiddish language.

Yiddish, of course, was still the language of the Jew, still very much the language of the ghetto, and in Mendelssohn's eyes the single reason most responsible for the Jew's continued alienation from the German host. Mendelssohn's ultimate goal was nothing short of integration of the German Jew into the culture and life of the German, while still maintaining the traditions and religious convictions of his forefathers. This was to be the new spirit, the new way. For Mendelssohn, the acceptance of the *Diaspora* was essential, the willingness to realize that the Jew must make some cultural accommodation with the modern world, must make a place for himself in society, while holding fast to those aspects of his religion which give him his peculiar identity as a Jew. All this could be possible, in Mendelssohn's view, if the Jew would only divest himself of that hateful and ugly language which tied him to the ghetto: Yiddish. Education was the key needed to open the lock, and to this end Mendelssohn embarked on a two-part program. In 1778, with his encouragement, the Jewish community of Berlin opened the Free Jewish School (*Jüdische Freischule*), with a curriculum which included German, Hebrew, Talmud, German secular literature, science, and mathematics. The language of instruction in all subjects was German. In 1783, Mendelssohn completed a translation of the Pentateuch into German; since few Jews had access to the German alphabet, he used the traditional Jewish linguistic method of phonetically transliterating with the Hebrew alphabet, writing from right to left. Still, when read aloud, the result was Mendelssohn's magnificent German; the text was accompanied by a Hebrew commentary.

The result of both these enormous intellectual innovations was predictable. The traditional rabbis were intensely disturbed, but they were not dealing with a charlatan or a pseudo-Messiah. Mendelssohn, by this time, had become not only a Jew to be reckoned with, but was one of the leading spirits of the century. The impact on Jewish life was perhaps measured in part by the Jewish historian Heinrich Graetz, who commented: "The inner freedom of the Jews dates from this translation." [2]

Almost with a swiftness which defies belief, the status, life style, and world of the German Jew had been permanently altered, in a way which Mendelssohn himself never envisioned. For his goals never changed. Mendelssohn wanted no more than a proper blend of modernism and tradition, and by tradition he meant the acceptance of those Jewish values which are the heart of patriarchal observance. He himself remained an Orthodox Jew until his death, fully following the laws and commandments. He did not apply the hard-headed reason of eighteenth-century Rationalism which marked the skepticism of much of the religious thinking emanating from enlightened men of the period. It was primarily in the sphere of social adjustment and cultural assimilation that he wished to modernize the Jew. Tragically, he did not realize that because of his fame, his name would inevitably be linked with religious reform as well.

The glory of Mendelssohn's accomplishments became both the glory and ultimate tragedy of German Jewry. Within a generation after his death, Mendelssohn's wish had become fact. Yiddish, as a language of communication, was almost dead in Germany, having been replaced for all purposes by German. The very next generation produced Heinrich Heine (1797–1856), destined to become the finest German lyric poet of the century; and within a century of Mendelssohn's death, Freud, Buber, and Einstein were writing in German, their native language. Every third Nobel Prize awarded to Germany was to be given to a German Jew whose basic research was conducted in German. The linguistic metamorphosis of that segment of the population proved to be one of the most spectacular accomplishments in the field of language acquisition which the modern age has seen.

But the triumph is irrevocably linked to tragedy. No sooner had Moses Mendelssohn shown his coreligionists the advantages of cultural assimilation than there began a wholesale race to the baptismal fonts of Berlin. For Mendelssohn, it was enough to be an assimilated German Jew; others preferred not to be a Jew at all. Heine's response to his liberation was typical: *"Mein Judentum ist mein Unglück"* (my Jewishness is my misfortune). Heine wanted access to fraternities at the universities, and in order to join, all he needed to do was to renounce his Judaism, a very minor step for the now fully assimilated young man who could, given the freedom which the age provided, pass for a German.

To pass for a German. This became a distinct possibility for all Jews who suddenly found themselves emancipated from the restrictions of the ghetto. For no sooner had Mendelssohn accomplished his task than events beyond Germany aided the Jewish cause. Napoleon breached the ghetto and tore it down. For him the emancipation of the Jew was essential to the emancipation of Europe. In spite of Metternich's hopes of returning to the old ways, the Jew was permanently free, part of Europe. Mendelssohn's own children, with one exception, abandoned his religion. German Jewry appeared in danger of complete disappearance. The attractions of Christianity were great, the advantages too obvious. Against these forces, the German rabbis responded with a series of reforms which, they hoped, would enable German Jews to maintain some aspect of their Jewish identity. From one end of Germany to the other, even in nonreforming congregations, German became the language of the rabbi's sermon, and more often of the prayer itself. Soon innovations were pouring into German Judaism in an effort to modernize and to hold onto the flock. Prayer books were revised to omit mention of the return to the Holy Land or references to Jewish national life. By the middle of the nineteenth century, the reform movement in Germany had sufficiently modernized and adjusted Judaism so as to make it identifiable with what today is called Reform Judaism. In its most radical form, Sunday services were substituted for the traditional Sabbath, and the service itself, with organ or instrumental music, men and women seated together, prayer in German, was indistinguishable from the Protestant service, which was the goal of many of the German Jewish reformers. They even gave themselves names other than that of Jew: Mosaite, Israelite, Semite. The model quite clearly was the Christian Church. The secular state was given the power which the rabbis formerly wielded.

German Jewry had adapted; beyond that, German Jewry had become something else, something ultimately its own. In their zeal to adhere to the spirit of Germany and to the identification with the German nation, then just experiencing its first sense of nationalism, the German Jews became, to a certain extent, more German than the Germans. They developed a distinct antipathy toward their fellow Jews, particularly to those who still held to the traditional pietism and, worse yet, language, of the old world. The German Jews simply would not acknowledge that they could speak or understand a word of Yiddish. Culturally, they were completely Germanized. Jews made up the inner circle of some of the most notorious Wagnerite and Teutophile groups. Some, in their misplaced zeal, became anti-Semites, making every effort to prevent the immigration of East European Jews into Germany. A gulf was created between the German Jew, assimilated, well bred, indistinguishable from the *Nationaldeutsche* (as Thomas Mann called them, to underline the difference he felt between the German and the Jew), and the "other" Jews, particularly those of the East, in their *shtetls,* speaking their Yiddish. The ultimate tragedy of German Jewry did not come about until the 1930s and the advent of Adolf Hitler. It seems almost inconceivable, but Hitler did manage to acquire 7 to 10 percent of the Jewish vote in elections from 1928 to 1933. When he raged against the "dirty Jew," there were always a few German Jews who simply could not accept the fact that Hitler meant them. Hitler *had* to be referring to *"die anderen,"* the other Jews from the East; and some of the German Jews wanted more or less the same thing as Hitler did at that time, *"eine Judensperre,"* a blockade against the Jews in the East.

In the end, the German Jew did relatively better at surviving than his East European brethren. Of the six hundred thousand pre-Hitler German Jews, including those whose hereditary background qualified them as Jews in spite of their protestations, over half managed to escape the Final Solution. But the shared experience of the Holocaust did not draw the German Jews closer to other survivors; the residue of that sense of separation will most likely never disappear. Fraternities at large American midwestern universities still have German-Jewish houses which simply as a matter of policy do not pledge the children of East Europeans. Even in Israel, there are still two kibbutzim where the language of daily discourse is German, and other languages are not encouraged. In the world of *yichus*, of Jewish status, the German Jew will always assume an extra measure for himself.

Hassidism

The Haskalah was an intellectual religious revolution. It produced the *maskil*, the man of the Enlightenment. He was educated, assimilated, a European. But at the very same moment in history, another religious revolution was taking place which let loose forces almost diametrically opposed to the *maskil* and everything that he represented. Yet the same conditions produced both events. Both revolutions were products of Jewish spiritual malaise, and were responses to it. Haskalah responded to the mind; Hassidism responded to the heart.

The roots of Hassidism go back to those very same forces which produced the false messianic fervor of the previous century. At the center was the medievalism of Kabbalistic thought, the mystery and spirituality of Jewish mysticism. This time, however, the result was not a spiritual entrepreneur like Shabbatai Zevi, but a genuine mystic whose impact was lasting far beyond the moment of Jewish travail. Little is known about the life of Israel ben Elizer (c. 1700–60), the founder of Hassidism. There are very few reliable historical documents of biography; he left behind no written material. Everything about him is surrounded by legend. He was born in the *shtetl* of Okup, in the Polish province of Podolia. Israel was not a particularly gifted student, but he gave himself up to the study of Kabbalah. He soon began a life as an itinerant healer and won a reputation as a miracle worker and curer of the sick and lame. He acquired the name Baal Shem Tov, Master of the Good Name, and his increasing band of followers called him *Besht*, a reverent abbreviation. Around 1745 he settled in the town of Medzhibozh in Podolia and opened a school, where instruction consisted almost exclusively of sitting at the Master's feet and listening to his teachings. Through the quiet power of his personality, the Baal Shem Tov made this academy one of the great centers of influence in the Jewish world.

The message was simple, intended for simple people. God is everywhere, and anyone has the power to approach Him. To approach the Divine Spirit, however, one must first be filled with the spirit of joyousness and confidence in the Almighty. Learning, while not rejected, was not necessary to attain divine experience. Any humble Jew, any *pintele Yid,* had access to God, as long as his heart was open and happy. This above all was essential, the banishment of sadness, of misery. The only path to heaven is one lined with singing and dancing angels, said the followers of the Baal Shem Tov. It was from these teachings that Hassidism acquired its unique sense of excitement and acceptance. Here was a movement, coming at a time when the Jew had sunk deep into the pits of damnation, that rejected sin, punishment, and retribution, and offered each Jew, no matter how rich or poor, the opportunity to dance his way to heaven. God could not be worshipped in sadness, so proclaimed the Baal Shem Tov and his disciples. Anything that produced pleasure was pleasing to God; the service of God through enjoyment, no matter how modest, was perhaps the most appealing aspect of the movement. Certainly the fact that modesty and humility were also pleasing to the heavenly spirit in the eyes of Hassidism also gave the wretched Jewish masses a strong sense of identification with Hassidic simplicity. The Hassidim always contrasted their ways and the arrogant sense of scholarship which the traditional orthodox rabbis suggested as the only proper attitude for leading the Jewish life. For the Hassidim, the cold, detached sectarianism of their opponents (called *Mitnagedim*) was diametrically opposed to the ecstatic fervor in prayer advocated by the Baal Shem Tov. Finally, it was this emotion which came to be the hallmark of Hassidic worship. Even today, at the gatherings of Hassidic groups (called *Farbrengenen*) one encounters the same outpouring of emotionalism, singing, dancing and joy at the encounter with the Divine Spirit.

The impact of the Baal Shem Tov's message was instantaneous. He was declared a saintly man, a *tzaddik,* by his followers, a mediator between man and God. His chief disciples spread the word throughout Poland and Russia, and Hassidism caught on almost immediately with the Jewish masses. The message was appropriate for the times, but above all, it was delivered in the correct language. For Hassidism was a movement of and for simple people, and the Baal Shem Tov understood how one communicates with these *pintele Yidn:* in their own language, in Yiddish. The language of Hassidism was from the very outset the language of the masses. All the Hassidic writings of the followers of the Baal Shem Tov were in the *mama-loshen.*

The generation of Hassidic leaders after the Baal Shem Tov turned Hassidism into a mass movement. Dov Ber of Meseritz (1710–72) was the appointed leader who spread the word of the Baal Shem Tov into the Ukraine. He also added, in his own teachings, certain refinements which changed the direction of the simple teachings of the Master. Dov Ber urged the people to seek out *tzaddikim,* those saintly people uniquely equipped to communicate with the Almighty. Thus, the person and power of the *tzaddik* became one of the special aspects of Hassidism, and ultimately led to its corruption. Within a few years, literally hundreds of miracle-working Hassidim, *wunder-rebbes,* had established themselves in Jewish communities all over the east of Europe. Some were genuinely gifted religious people, others were charlatans and profiteers who, taking advantage of their charismatic powers, attracted large numbers of followers who would come to their "courts" in order to share a piece of matzoh at Passover or to get a brief audience with the *rebbe*. Eventually, the person of each *tzaddik* became the center of a personality cult. The sense of joyousness advocated by the Baal Shem Tov was corrupted by the unscrupulous into an occasional grossness which shocked other genuine Hassidim. Some of the *tzaddikim* lived in royal splendor and wealth, provided by their worshipping followers. Inevitably, such excesses led to a desire to maintain control over the population, and it became the custom to assert that the *tzaddik's* powers could be handed down to his descendants. As a result, a system of hereditary transmission of "the divine spark" made the entire movement dynastic.

Perhaps the greatest impact of the movement was in the South, particularly in the Ukraine, where more than half of the Jewish masses belonged to the Hassidic community. Living in even greater misery and ignorance, these huddled Jewish masses discovered a new faith in Judaism, and in their belief in the powers of their *tzaddikim* they discovered an intimate, personal relationship with God which brought some ray of hope into their desperate lives. The opponents of Hassidism did everything they could to demonstrate the un-Jewish nature of the movement; in the north of Poland and Russia particularly, the strong anti-Hassidic sentiment of the rabbis led them to ask the official governmental authorities to investigate the Hassidim. Jew turned on Jew, and the resultant bitterness and hatred of the *Litvak* in the face of Hassidism left its mark on Jewish society for generations. Today, one might hear a passing remark, intended as humorous, made to a child: "Remember, after all, your father is a Litvak." A hundred years ago a daughter of a Hassidic family who married a Litvak might cause an irreconcilable split in the family. It was serious business.

The center of anti-Hassidic activity was Vilna, and the leading enemy of Hassidism was Rabbi Elijah ben Solomon Zalman (1720–1797), the *Gaon* (a term of honor) of Vilna, who in 1772 issued a ban of excommunication against Hassidic followers. This did not prevent Hassidism from penetrating to his very doorstep. A Hassidic group was established in the Lithuanian town of Lyady, not far from Vilna itself, under the leadership of Rabbi Shneour Zalman (1748–1813). This remarkable intellectual understood that in order for Hassidism to succeed in the more skeptical, educated North, it required a refinement, a blending of the mind with the heart, in order to give it a character which, while maintaining the emotional and intimate quality of Hassidism, provided some of the solid erudition of orthodoxy. The result was a new kind of Hassidism, with a theoretical system, that nevertheless maintained the exuberance of the old. Shneour Zalman moved the court to the neighboring town of Lubavitch, which gave its name to the Hassidic group known today the world over as the Lubavitcher Hassidim, the most successful, perhaps the most modern, and certainly the most accommodating of all the sects. Today, the Lubavitcher movement is distinctly international in scope, ranging all over the globe in an effort to locate and to confront fallen-away Jews who might be susceptible to a modernized version of traditional faith.[3]

By the mid-nineteenth century, Hassidism had splintered and deteriorated. Many *tzaddikim* began to urge a synthesis of Hassidic values and principles with the teachings of the Baal Shem Tov and traditional rabbinical scholarship. Out of this activity came the image of Hassidism which is common in our age, namely, as the bulwark of reactionary orthodoxy. The original gentle, flexible, and joyous approach to faith taken by the Baal Shem Tov has evolved into a fragmented movement, further decimated by the Nazi Holocaust, but still based on the principles of dynastic inheritance. The single most characteristic aspect of some of the present-day Hassidic sects is narrow sectarianism and reactionary exclusiveness. The Satmar Hassidim of Williamsburg, Brooklyn, for instance, under the leadership of the Teitelbaum family, refer to all other Jews, even other Hassidim, as *goyim*, Gentiles, fallen from the true ways. They take a most literal interpretation of the Bible, adhering strictly to every rule and directive of orthodox law. They view the efforts of the Lubavitcher Hassidim to reach out to other Jews as heretical.

In the closing decades of the nineteenth century, Hassidism had a strong grip on the Jewish population of the Pale of Settlement. It had by this time taken a position which had both ideological as well as religious implications. Considering itself the ultimate representative of what it saw as the Jewish tradition, Hassidism was determined to keep out the modern world, which its leaders saw as threatening the values of the Jewish world of the Pale. We find, then, three forces at work as the century draws to a close: the Haskalah, begun in Germany, and specifically in Berlin, did make an eastern passage, did find some acceptance in Eastern Europe, but particularly in the North, in Lithuania, where the better educated and more receptive Jewish community could be found. The Vilna Gaon, as early as the 1770s, had urged some of his followers to read Mendelssohn's works and to understand the importance of secular education. There were *maskilim* in Eastern Europe, but of course their language of intellectual discourse was either Russian, if they could learn it, or Polish, but most often Hebrew. The Haskalah in the East was associated with the regeneration of Hebrew as a literary language. Like Mendelssohn, these modern thinkers wanted no part of the hated Yiddish jargon, which they too recognized as the language of the ghetto, of the past, and of reactionary Hassidism.

The other force was that of the *Mitnagedim*, the orthodox but non-Hassidic rabbinical traditionalists who were willing to make an accommodation with the modern world, but who totally rejected the heresies which they saw in Hassidism. They allied themselves more with the Haskalah out of mutual hatred of the Hassidim, who increasingly were becoming the unmovable traditionalists.

The Hassidim, massed primarily in the South, and controlling the largest number of Jews, fought for the maintenance of the old ways, in customs, in attitudes, and, finally, in traditional religious orthodoxy, which they had fused to the mysticism of the Baal Shem Tov's teachings.

What was the prize? The hearts and minds of millions of Jews, living in a kind of medieval suspension. In Poland, the situation was somewhat better, because the governments had reluctantly dragged the Jewish population into the modern world, or at least had dragged them into it to the same degree as the rest of the Polish population. In the Austro-Hungarian empire, the Jewish population had for decades enjoyed some civil liberties. Even as far back as the days of Maria Theresa, the Jews had taken Germanized names because the Empress insisted on it when the first census was taken.[4]

But the situation for the Russian Jew was vastly different. Since the 1790s, when Catherine the Great acquired a large Jewish population from Poland, the Pale of Settlement had officially existed. Jews were required to live in restricted areas, with limited rights of travel and occupation. After a temporary improvement during the Napoleonic threat, matters got worse when Nicholas I became Czar in 1825. A violent anti-Semite, Nicholas was the first of the modern European rulers who tried to solve his Jewish problem. His hopes were that one-third would die, one-third would convert, and the rest would emigrate. In order to facilitate the conversion, Nicholas instituted a special Jewish draft into the military, which forced Jews into service for twenty-five years. During this period, the forces of Haskalah and non-Hassidic orthodoxy could do little to help the Jewish population adjust to the modern world, since there was hardly any cooperation from the authorities. Hassidism flourished within this spirit of reactionary governmental oppression.

But when Nicholas I died and Alexander II assumed the throne of Russia in 1855, another revolution began which altered the entire course of Jewish history, and profoundly altered the course of Haskalah, of Hassidism, indeed of world history, for Jew and Gentile alike.

3

East European Jewry in Crisis: The Threat of the Modern Age

 It was the ascension of Alexander II to power which first threatened the hold of Hassidism over the Jews of Eastern Europe, for this genuinely liberal monarch encouraged the *maskilim* and the forward-looking orthodox to think that the Jewish population was about to enter an age of progress. Indeed, Alexander II's policies provided the Jews with an atmosphere of freedom that had been completely unknown to them. He abolished most of the anti-Semitic restrictions of his predecessor, relaxed the residency regulations in the Pale, permitted the Jews freedom of movement, and provided Jewish writers and journalists with the opportunity to communicate with the Jewish masses.

The problem for the Jewish writer, however, was that he did not know how to communicate. In 1856, the first Hebrew journal to be published in Russia appeared, with a potential readership of four and one-half million. Its circulation never went above two thousand. The *maskilim* were eager to print the events of the modern world, they hastened to bring information concerning the impact of technology, science, religious reform, progress on all fronts, to the Jews huddled in their *shtetls,* but they insisted on using a language that these masses simply did not have access to. The fact was that Jews, the ordinary Jews of Russia, did not read literary Hebrew. Very few could read Russian or Ukrainian. The Jew had one language, Yiddish, and for the *maskil,* whether he was totally assimilated, religiously progressive, or orthodox, Yiddish was not a fit language for communication. In 1862, a Yiddish supplement to the Hebrew journal was reluctantly agreed to, but the language of the occasional Yiddish issue was kept deliberately elevated, highly Germanized, and aloof.

None of the Jewish intellectuals who were concerned with reaching the masses felt any need to communicate in Yiddish, particularly because it appeared that, given the relaxation of persecution under Alexander, the hoped-for assimilation, integration, and adjustment of Jewish life in Russia to a more modern style would inevitably take place. Even Hassidism, with its suspicions of modernism and its hatred of change from the traditional ways of the past, could not survive without the tensions, without the persecution. Indeed, Hassidism seemed to flourish most when the Jew needed to turn within himself, to bury his roots even deeper into traditional Jewish soil. The language of this arch-conservatism, as the *maskilim* saw it, was Yiddish, and this, too, was destined to disappear in the age of liberalism. The message of the *maskilim,* and of the Hebrew press which the age of Alexander II created, was one of adjustment, of flexibility, of increased optimism. The Hebrew writers, although they recognized that they were not really reaching the masses, felt no pressure to do so, since it appeared to be only a question of time before the walls of reaction would be breeched.

But the euphoria ended almost as quickly as it had begun. In the spring of 1881, Alexander II was assassinated, probably by those who feared his liberal views, and he was replaced on the throne by Alexander III, who can be described as the most anti-Semitic modern ruler to appear before the rise of Adolf Hitler. By late spring Alexander was ready to act against the Jews, and he instituted the notorious May Laws of 1881, which marked the return of the Jew to a state of even greater medieval bondage. The Pale was reinstituted, more repressively than ever. Restrictions on Jewish trade and mobility produced harsh disruptions; entire families were uprooted, and orders came down forcing Jewish villages to move overnight to other locations, now defined as geographic ghettoes on an enormous scale. Where Jews had lived for centuries, now no Jew could reside.

Perhaps those most crushed by the sudden shift in the atmosphere were the optimistic intellectuals who had sincerely believed that the Jew was on the verge of a new epoch in Czarist Russia. But now the message was clear: get out. Furthermore, the message had to be spread with an increasing urgency, for it was apparent to those who were at least able to perceive the forces and changes which the late years of the century were producing that, unless something dramatic took place, the Jewish millions were going to be caught under someone's grinding wheels. Change was going to have to come about, whether the masses, the Hassidim, the traditionalists liked it or not. And it was going to be the task of the Jewish intellectuals to bring this message to the people, to the hundreds of little *shtetl* communities which had existed for centuries in their traditional customs and ways, rocked occasionally by a cataclysmic event like a pogrom, but generally unchanged, and for the most part unwilling to change.

Initially, it fell to the intellectual to get the word of Alexander III's persecutions out to the public, to the Jewish public. The new pressures, the disruptions and dislocations had been felt in almost every Russian *shtetl,* so it was clear to the Jews that something not particularly beneficial was taking place. However, the *shtetl* Jew had lived in his private isolation even when the liberal spirit was alive in the land.

The World of the Shtetl

The typical Jewish Russian *shtetl* contained perhaps one hundred to one thousand Jews. A Jewish *shtetl* within a big city, a ghetto or a large Jewish quarter such as one might find in Vilna, Bialystok, or Kiev, could have many thousands. But in the provinces of Vilna, Mohilev, Grodno, Minsk in the north, or Volhynia, Kiev, and Poltava at the northern reach of the Ukraine, to Podolia and Bessarabia in the south, one could find hundreds of villages with Jewish communities, most of which have since been blotted off the map. The larger *shtetls* (Skvira, Bratzlav, Bar, Lyady, Lubavitch, Mezritch, Berdichev, Zhitomir, Slutsk, Shklov, Karlin, Mir[1]) still recall the past glories of great Hassidic rabbis and their followers. But whether you were a follower of the Skvira Rebbe or the Bratzlaver, the value system was the same. The Jewish *shtetl* world was a self-contained one that was definable in its own terms and traditions. To understand it and then to penetrate it, one had to understand the nature of religious and social orders as the *shtetl* inhabitants regarded them. Religion, particularly, dominated every aspect of life. You were defined in terms of your attitude toward your faith, whether you were a pious Jew or a nonbeliever. No matter what, you were a Jew. Simply not attending synagogue services or, more aggressively, pronouncing your atheism, was not sufficient to keep others from accepting your Jewish identity any more than it kept the individual doing the denying from accepting it. A Jew was a Jew in the *shtetl*. Of course, the vast majority were practicing Jews, generally Hassidic. The language of the *shtetl* was clearly and almost exclusively Yiddish. The dominating thought of weekly life was living for the Sabbath, for *Shabbes*, for the one day when the miserable life of poverty could be forgotten. In most *shtetls*, the main occupation was begging. The *shnorrer*, the Jewish beggar, often made up one-third of a *shtetl* population.[2] During the bad times of Jewish oppression and restrictions on occupations, life in the *shtetl*

43

was desperate. There was simply not enough means of economic gain to provide food for the inhabitants. Thus the quest for *parnosseh*, a living, a means for providing for family and the Sabbath meal, dominated the thoughts of the wretched villager. How you made your *parnosseh*, your status in the community, your location in the synagogue in relation to the rabbi's seat, how much you might be able to give to charity, to provide for those even more wretched than yourself, these were the preoccupations of the *shtetl* inhabitant. For in a world where existence was marginal, where the very rich might be separated from the very poor only by the possession of a coat or a garment to wear on the Sabbath or holiday, these were the substantial facts of existence. As a result, *yichus,* your rank or status, in both social and religious terms, was of the utmost importance. At the top, with more *yichus* than anyone, was the revered rabbi, the ultimate arbiter of *shtetl* life, the one who determined if the chicken was healthy, if the wife could leave her husband, if a rule of Jewish life had been violated. He possessed knowledge, perhaps the most highly treasured commodity of *shtetl* life. He had studied Torah, and this earned the rabbi a special measure of respect in the community. Learning was treasured, and Jewish learning treasured above everything. If you happened to have some wealth, it was not bad, either. The rich man of the *shtetl,* the *nogid,* was beneath the rabbi in respect, in *yichus,* but he was able to acquire those aspects of learning which were valuable and honored, and which might even provide him with greater status. For example, if he were rich enough, he could look for a potential son-in-law from the great Yeshivas, the centers of Jewish learning, and find a young man gifted in scholarship for his daughter. Then he would be performing one of the great deeds, one of the great commandments—*mitzvot*—of Judaism, to encourage learning. The *nogid* would "keep" his son-in-law, would provide all the means required to survive, so long as he continued his studies. Having a "kept" son-in-law who continued to study Torah brought even greater honor to the nogid. The responsibilities of being the wealthy man of the Jewish community were great. The strongest of traditions required that the rich provide for the poor, and often the nogid was reluctant to share his hard-earned gains with what he often perceived to be free-loaders. Still, at Passover, the dispensation of matzos to the poor was the obligation of the nogid (or negidim, if there was more than one rich man in the shtetl) and the esteem he enjoyed was directly proportionate to his generosity and good will.

The nogid's wife was the envy of all the women of the shtetl, because she above all others possessed the status and honor of rank. Her husband could provide her with the yichus which others failed to furnish. The vast majority of Jewish women in the community did not have the status which they wished to possess, and because of the attitude toward learning, they were unable to acquire status in any other way. For the Jewish female, by tradition, stopped studying at a very young age, perhaps eight or nine, and it was left exclusively to the young Jewish boy to continue with the study of Torah. One of the oft-repeated sayings of the shtetl was: "When the hen begins to crow like a rooster, it's time to take it to the shoychet" (the religious ritual slaughterer). In scholarly terms this meant that it was an unnatural act for a female to study like a male. Jewish women were not provided with the opportunity—that was the way of the shtetl. At best, a woman might read some translations of the learned book in Yiddish and fulfilled, if possible, her greatest task: to provide a Jewish home for her family and to give her husband the leisure to pursue the life of learning.[3] When the economics of shtetl life allowed it, the women more often assumed the major money-earning tasks, in order to give their husbands time for serious scholarly activities. Needless to say, the greatest part of the shtetl inhabitants was so thoroughly impoverished that this ideal situation did not occur as frequently as the habitual poverty that prevented the average male Jew from indulging in the life of Torah. Instead, the normal Jewish male worked himself to the bone, and if he were lucky, he might find a few moments to read in one of the great books. His Hebrew had deteriorated, but he could still manage, perhaps, a bit of Rashi's commentaries. The woman worked alongside the male, frequently bitter at her state, cursing her life if she became depressed enough, often venting her anger and frustration on her husband.

Marriages in the *shtetl* were not usually affairs of the heart. Matches were inevitably arranged by parents and the matchmaker, the *shadchan,* without the consent or the knowledge of the young people involved. The average age of engaged couples was somewhere around thirteen or fourteen. Usually, the young post-Bar Mitzvah youth would be told by his father that he was to be congratulated. Within a few weeks he would meet an equally uninformed young girl, his future wife. Perhaps a year or two later they would meet again, at the wedding ceremony.

Beyond anything else, the family, the concept of *mishpoche* in Hebrew and Yiddish, the sense of kinship, dominated *shtetl* society. Within this world, the relationship between parent and child was at the center of life. The sole purpose of the parent was to produce children who would bring *yichus* to the family and a sense of gratification, pleasure, and esteem as well. The pleasure derived from children was called *naches;* the honor and esteem, *koved.* The male child could provide honor for the family by being a talented student, primarily.[4] A female child offered less promise to the family, but there was always the possibility of a good marriage. Children were of course loved, but they were also beaten. The *shtetl* world did not deal particularly in child psychology. At the age of three a boy, not much more than an infant, was sent off to study with a teacher who quite

46

regularly might brutalize him. For the adolescent engaged couple, not yet fully developed teenagers, there was little in the way of sex education. There was only one cardinal rule: do not dishonor the family.

Within this frame of reference, most behavior was acceptable. To get too much of a sunburn suggested that a young man might not be studying enough, for which he could receive a cuff on the ear and the admonishment not to be *goyish*. In the old country, the most physically desirable male type was that associated with the student: thin and pale. If one appeared too robust and healthy, it was a sign of non-Jewish behavior. It might also lead a young man to acts which might also be described as Gentile, acts of physical violence which most *shtetl* Jews had by tradition been educated to seeing as non-Jewish. Talmudic conditioning for the entire two thousand years of the Diaspora urged the Jew to adopt a passive posture when it came to his own defense. Survival in exile became associated with nonaggression, and for centuries Jews would permit themselves to be burned, murdered, and otherwise assaulted in an enduring persecution. The spirit of the ghetto was one which told the Jew to hide if possible, but that it was futile to attempt to raise your fist in defense, and furthermore, that it was against the strictures of the Talmud. Whatever arguments might have been brought forth by more strident and forceful people through the ages, the pacifist attitude clearly dominated, and this feeling was widespread throughout the *shtetl* we are now describing.

The Gentile might be violent, but not the Jew. In fact, the *goy* was capable of all sorts of excesses in the eyes of the Jewish community. For him was reserved all the stereotyping which Gentile communities had envisioned when creating the image of the Jew. For the Jew, the Gentile generally meant the local peasant. If relations with the surrounding communities were good, then there were cordial feelings on all sides.

Some Gentiles served the Jewish congregation on the Sabbath, and during the Nazi occupation of Poland and Russia there were endless stories of heroic deeds done by friendly peasants who courageously hid Jews from the Gestapo and Wehrmacht. But traditionally the *goy* was for the Jew a lower type, less educated, often a drunkard who beat his wife, and who on occasion could get violent and ugly. Above all, he was ignorant, possessed a *goyishe kop,* a Gentile head. Association with Gentiles was strongly discouraged, because it might lead to the only acts which were unacceptable on any account: apostasy, conversion to Christianity, or marriage to a Gentile. The *shtetl* Jew was not interested in gaining converts to Judaism. Marrying a Gentile who was willing to convert to Judaism was the same as marrying a Gentile who was not: it was still marriage to a *shiksa,* a Gentile girl, or a *shaygits,* a Gentile boy, and as such a sure way to dishonor the family. Official conversion, in order to make the quota for the Russian university, for example, meant that your name was struck from the Jewish rolls of the community, and for Jews this meant that you were officially dead. That was the rigid ethical response of the family and the community, for whom the loss of a member of the *shtetl* was no different and no less real than an actual death.

The Shtetl World and the Modern World

Into this world which had remained relatively unchanged for centuries started pressing, in the last decades of the nineteenth century, those ideas and forces which helped change the face of Europe and the world: the various "isms" have been accounted for in nearly every textbook on the subject of the Modern Age. But for the Jew, who had had little preparation for either the technology or the events of the age, the shock was greater than for other peoples. Socialism, racism, nationalism, and, unique for the Jew, Zionism, quite suddenly and dramatically had become powerful ideas which now threatened this traditional world which the Jew, in spite of the misery, and even in spite of the recurring threats of the anti-Semitic Czar, had grown accustomed to. The isolation of the *shtetl* was considerable, and, as we shall see when we consider the efforts of Yiddish writers to penetrate it, the older generation particularly showed no great desire to discover what the outside world had to offer. Moreover, the leaders of the Jewish communities could see the potential mischief in the intrusion of new ideas, which to them led only to one thing: assimilation and the ultimate disappearance of the Jewish people. The Hassidim as well as many of the orthodox *mitnaggedim* looked with great concern at the events and revolutions going on around them.

But the Jewish intellectuals, the *maskilim* and orthodox thinkers who understood the implications of these events, of the formation of Jewish socialist workers' groups in the cities, of the Dreyfus trial, of Herzl's ideas, of the crackpot eugenic theories of race current in France and Germany, these thinkers realized that somehow the message had to be brought to the *shtetl* inhabitant. The only question was: how to do it?

Mendele Mocher Sforim

Inevitably, someone had to take the first step. The unique historical moment had come for the Jews, and what was needed now was a chronicler or a bearer of tidings. The fact that the Hebrew literary renaissance had failed to have any great impact on *shtetl* life was apparent to those Hebrew writers and journalists who had been active in the establishment of the first Hebrew language journal in Russia. They also noted the increased interest when, in 1862, the first Yiddish supplement to that journal appeared. One of these writers, Sholom Abramovitch (1836–1917), himself a noted

49

maskil with a reputation as a serious writer of Hebrew articles in the prominent journals, took that initial step, which was no small risk. Any serious Hebrew publicist caught writing in the "jargon," in Yiddish, could damage his reputation beyond repair, so ridiculed was Yiddish as a means of important literary potential. Therefore Abramovitch, before publishing his Yiddish story *Dos kleyne Menshele* ("The Little Man") in the Yiddish supplement *Kol Mevaser* of the Hebrew journal *Hamelitz,* decided on a safeguard: he would hide his identity behind a pseudonym. Every *shtetl* and big-city ghetto recognized the figure of the itinerant book peddler, whose pushcart appeared regularly with a variety of prayer books, shawls, and other liturgical items. Abramovitch came up with the name *Mendele Mocher Sforim,* Mendele the Book Peddler. In his Hebrew writings, Abramovitch was a Jewish muckraker, denouncing restrictive educational practices in the *shtetl* and narrowminded Jewish parochialism, attacking the hypocrisy of a Jewish society which supposedly took care of its poor but which in fact, he stated, did little of the kind.

Dos kleyne Menshele appeared in the November 1863 issue, and Mendele continued in Yiddish what he had won his reputation for in Hebrew, but the impact was as enormous as it was dramatic. The thirty-page story is about a cunning and devious *shtetl* Jew who learns how to exploit rich and poor to gain his fortune. Toward the end of his life, he repents and the major part of the story is taken up with the reading of his will, just before his death. *Dos kleyne Menshele* tells how he became the wretched human being he is; first, he was a much-abused orphan beaten and maltreated by the system of Jewish education; then, he learned from the Jewish community leaders how to be a proper parasite, hiding behind a cloak of righteousness and piety. Mendele set the tone for Yiddish literature with this story, which was to be one of the hallmarks of the tradition for a century, a tradition that continued unaltered when the linguistic metamorphosis into English took place in America. Mendele's story is an attack on hypocrisy, a dissection of the social foibles of "the haves" who live at the expense of "the have-nots." It is a biting critical analysis of social and family life in the Jewish community. No sooner had the supplement carrying the story appeared than the journal was besieged with requests for more of Mendele. Issues of the paper had been handed around until they were in tatters. Mendele was the potential, and the short story became a serialized novel, chronicling the further adventures of the little man, the new Jewish antihero.

Mendele-Abramovitch's contribution as the founder of serious Yiddish literature cannot be overstated. As a writer, he had many shortcomings, to be sure. The didactic quality of his narrative leads more often than not to over-kill. He can be shrilly moralistic, often without humor, and hammers away with a sense of moral outrage that on occasion leaves the modern reader somewhat numb. But the heavy-handed satire was perhaps exactly what the potential reader needed, and Mendele fully understood the psychological make-up of his audience. Abramovitch completely disappears and places the story in the hands of Mendele the Bookseller. The artless and folksy tone of this typical *shtetl* figure carries the narrative forward and into the minds of the reader. Mendele is the frame of the story around which the social criticism is built. Throughout, however, is the outrage of the *maskil*, denouncing misplaced *yichus*, petty Jewish pride and vanity, and urging the communities to look after their poor.

The Yiddish literary revolution was underway. In *Die Takse* ("The Meat Tax"), Mendele turns his attack on the Jewish community's rich, the *negidim*, who oppress the poor and keep them in a state of ignorance of the world around them. Mendele creates the imaginary *shtetl* of Glupsk and populates it with a stupid array of superstitious Jewish types. Finally, the poor find a leader, a *maskil* named *Veker* (literally "The Waker") who attempts to enlighten his fellow Jews. He is a genuine social protester and reformer. But the people cannot break away from the oppressive chains of orthodoxy, and the spiritual rebellion fails. The inhabitants of Glupsk were the inhabitants of those countless *shtetls* throughout the Pale. Mendele simply described them in terms recognizable to every reader. There were the greedy rich, the pious frauds, gentle rabbis, *shlemihls* and *shlimmazels,* the hard luck but still smiling wretches who manage to survive;[5] the *luftmensh,* the tragic Jew made out of air (the Yiddish meaning is "man of air") and suspended in midair, unable to rest his feet on the earth or to stretch his hands to heaven, the ultimate economic victim of Jewish life in the Pale. He becomes the economic parasite of the *shtetl,* dealing in nothing to make a living, the hustler, the pitiful and desperately driven Jew in search of "a killing."

In *Die Klatshe* ("The Broken-Down Horse"), Mendele began his full-fledged assault on *shtetl* sensibility. This is a satirical allegory which presents the Jewish people as a prince bewitched and turned into a broken-down nag. The horse is beaten, abused, and persecuted. In spite of this, the old horse maintains its dignity and rises above its misery. Within the narrative there is also the story of a young Jew named Zippe who wants to study medicine at the university. He is attacked by the Jewish elders and accused of spreading heretical ideas with his desire for secular learning. In this one story Mendele combines the sense of Jewish nationalism and pride along with an explicit call for modernization; indeed, Zippe is finally urged to leave his *shtetl* behind and to seek his future elsewhere.

Mendele continued to exhort the Jew to face the future. *Fishke the Lame* is a novel of utter Jewish poverty; *The Travels and Adventures of Benjamin the Third* takes its hero on a Don Quixote-like series of adventures through *shtetls* of the Pale; *The Wishing Ring (Dos Vinshfingeril)* represents

Mendele's most outspoken declamation of the end of the *shtetl* world. This is a panoramic novel about a Jewish *maskil* named Hershele who first experiences the euphoria of the pre-1881 days and looks longingly toward the time of Jewish assimilation in Russia; but after the May Laws he has a reawakening to Jewish identity, and realizes the uselessness of integration in a hostile society. Hershele looks for hope elsewhere, outside of Russia.

Between 1862 and the end of the century, Mendele-Abramovitch accomplished a remarkable feat. He had, first of all, provided respectability for writing in Yiddish, he had literally made it possible to be taken seriously as a Yiddish literary personality. Even more important, however, he had created a reading public. Within a matter of a few short years after he had begun writing in Yiddish, a publishing industry had sprung up which made cheap editions of Yiddish works available to millions of people who had never been reached before. Instead of book peddlers appearing in each *shtetl* with the traditional religious objects to sell, one now could purchase for a few kopeks a story or novel by Mendele. One copy would circulate through dozens of hands, until the print had vanished. The readers hardly thought that they were reading fiction. Mendele's sense of *shtetl* life was thoroughly accurate; he understood the *shtetl*, knew its inhabitants, even though he himself was a cultured man of letters. He opened the door of the *shtetl* world to ideas. It remained for another to penetrate that world right down to its roots.

4

Sholom Aleichem's Tevye Stories: The Crisis of Family Life

THE first readers of Mendele's fiction were admittedly not sophisticated members of the literary intelligentsia. They were remarkably similar to the people they were reading about. Eventually, some criticism of Mendele's constant harping and aggressive moralizing was heard; letters to *Kol Mevaser* were uniformly enthusiastic about this new voice for the masses, but occasionally a note crept in which suggested that perhaps a bit more sympathy for the people might be in order. It was this sense of compassion, the ability to empathize, which secured a position totally unique in the hearts of the Yiddish reading public for the next and perhaps most representative writer which the literature produced.

Like Mendele, Sholom Rabinovitch (1859–1916) was a *maskil*. He was born in Pereyaslav, Ukraine, a medium-sized town with a sizeable Jewish population, but as an infant he moved with his family to Voronko, a genuine Ukrainian *shtetl*, where he was brought up. Rabinowitz, however, was able to secure a public high school education, learned Russian, married well, and acquired considerable secular knowledge although recognized as a *Rabbiner*, a state-appointed Rabbi not particularly admired by the Jewish communities. Rabinovitch was a bona fide Jewish intellectual who, like his contemporaries, was committed to the Hebrew language for serious discourse. But the considerable success of Mendele proved to be the needed impetus for other Hebrew-writing *maskilim* to go public as Yiddishists. Still, there was the risk of destroying a hard-won reputation, and the recently married Sholom Rabinovitch was not about to take such a chance. He, like Mendele, selected a pseudonym which his potential reading audience could immediately identify with, a phrase literally on the lips of every Yiddish-speaking Jew every day of his life, the salutation "Sholom Aleichem," used by the Jew to welcome and to say goodbye. Yiddish literature, strangely, still refused to come out of the closet. Its two most influential figures were unable to write under their real names out of fear of damaging their prestige.

From the publication of his first Yiddish story, *Tsvey Shteiner* ("Two Stones"), in 1882, Sholom Aleichem was to become a name synonymous with all that was characteristic of Yiddish literature, both as a literary and a folk form. With the development of the works of this unique talent, we encounter the perfect blending of subject, form, and message which allows an instantaneous and total identification of a literature and those people who make up the audience. Mendele's targets were many, his exposure of the foibles of *shtetl* life could be so sharp as to lack sympathy. Sholom Aleichem almost exclusively pointed his attention to the one aspect of *shtetl* life he knew represented its most important entity: the family. He sensed that with the disintegration of Jewish life amidst the upheavals that seemed to be shaking the Jewish world, family life, with all its traditions and values, would have to undergo a shuddering change as it moved into the modern age. This above all else made Sholom Aleichem unique among Yiddish writers. With the publication of a story entitled "The Penknife" (*Dos Messerl*) in 1886, Sholom Aleichem consciously identified his fictional world with that of the conflicting generations of old and young Jews as the *shtetl* faced an uncertain future—what Irving Howe, in describing the phenomenon of Jewish-American literature, calls a focus on "the continuities, pains and rebellions of urban family life." [1] "The Penknife" ushered in a new theme for Yiddish literature, at a time when this literature had just begun to discover a sociology all its own. In this story the focus becomes sharper, the theme narrower. We are concentrating now on the struggle of the generations, the theme which was to mark Sholom Aleichem's fiction and which ultimately set the course for the development of the peculiarly Jewish contribution to American literature as well. The story is about a *shtetl* boy's love for knives, a preoccupation which a strict and orthodox father sees as mere frivolity. The father is absorbed in his studies, indifferent to the youthful enthusiasms of his son. Flights of fancy are paid back with beatings and abuse. The absorption with knives as playthings appears to threaten the existence of the patriarch, who tries to beat his son into studying. The picture of the *cheder*, the Jewish parochial school, is devastating. Sadistic teachers whip the children. The young lad finds his only satisfaction in improvising makeshift penknives, until one day he is tempted into stealing a magnificent one from a German who is staying as a guest at his parents' inn. The guilt-riddled young thief becomes feverish and hallucinates, and for two weeks he is bedridden in a state of semiconsciousness. Finally he awakens, to the relief of his parents, who have tried every remedy known to Jewish folklore to rid their son of the evil eye. As he returns from his deep sleep, the young boy is himself overjoyed, "so that he could have kissed his father. But how can one possibly kiss one's father?" [2]

Even from the point of view of literary form and technique, "The Penknife" surpassed anything that Mendele had written in Yiddish before it. The father's constant coughing echoes like a Dickensian leit-motif through the conflict. The story is told by the son, as an adult, as he reflects back on an unhappy childhood. Reminiscence of a Jewish childhood became Sholom Aleichem's most familiar narrative form.

Indeed, it seemed inevitable that the theme of generational conflict and family disintegration would capture the attention of the Yiddish writer, because events after 1881 made it perfectly clear that a disruption of unbelievable proportions was about to take place. It did not take long for the message of the *maskilim,* in Yiddish and Hebrew, to penetrate to the *shtetl.* Events in Russia made it all too clear that the old world was doomed. Pogroms, anti-Jewish laws, a whole new series of persecutions and dislocations got the message through: leave. Assisted by Jewish welfare agencies all over Europe, almost at once hundreds of Jewish families began a trek across the continent which frequently left them separated from loved ones, a separation which often became permanent. It was the younger generation particularly which interpreted the spirit of the times to mean that the one world was coming to an end and that the new one was about to be born. It was this youthful, courageous generation which picked up roots and searched for the Promised Land—in America. The voluntary Jewish relief organizations would often provide the thirty dollars for transatlantic passage, as long as the emigrants could get themselves to the seaports and pass the test for glaucoma, the eye disease which authorities believed at that time to be too infectious to allow its sufferers into the United States.

This was an end and a beginning. It represented the first trickling which ultimately was to become a flood of Jewish immigration to America from Czarist Russia, and later from Poland. It also represented the beginning of the actual breakdown of the *shtetl* world which Hitler ultimately destroyed, but which surely was in a serious state of disintegration by the time the Holocaust took place.

It fell to Sholom Aleichem to understand fully the meaning and scope of this crisis. He saw the inevitable generational struggle, the converging of forces which could not exist side by side, and he understood the unavoidable tragedy of these events. He saw that in the literature of the Jews one might find the proper vehicle to chronicle this conflict, and his genius created the representative Jewish Everyman who was forced to confront these events. In Tevye the Dairyman, Sholom Aleichem created a perfect *shtetl pintele Yid,* a small-town little Jew, in the midst of a conflagration he does not understand. The *shtetl* is breaking up, the outside world is penetrating Tevye's traditional world, and out of this conflict will emerge the next generation of Jews who, unlike Tevye, are willing to face the new world and its adventures. Tevye is as real as any Jewish *shtetl* type, and it was this reality which made him an instant folk hero for Sholom Aleichem's readers. Sholom Aleichem wrote nine Tevye stories over a period of fifteen years, from 1892 to 1907, and these short, artless narratives reveal as no other body of literature the nature of the disaster which beset Jewish family life, as Sholom Aleichem attempts to communicate with his audience what the disruption was to mean to European Jewry. Sholom Aleichem himself was experiencing the very same injuries which were to befall Tevye. The pogroms in Kishinev in 1903 left him convinced that the Jewish presence in Russia was over. In 1906 he made his first exploratory visit to the United States and returned to Europe. While he never returned to his homeland to live,[3] he traveled throughout Europe until the events of the First World War overwhelmed him and his family. After a brief internment in Germany and then Denmark he managed to find refuge in America. The great tragedy of Sholom Aleichem's later years was the death of his son, Misha, who had remained in Denmark. Sholom Aleichem himself died in America, in 1916. He was buried at Mount Nebo Cemetery, in Brooklyn, New York. Hundreds of thousands of mourners lined the funeral route. Maurice Samuel, who attended the funeral, wrote later: "Why, then, should

they not mourn? Who was to speak for them now that
Sholom Aleichem was dead, and who was to remember them
if he was forgotten?" [4]

Samuel expressed a sentiment shared by Sholom Aleichem's
millions of Yiddish-speaking readers all over the world, but
particularly in Russia and later in America, and no one more
than Tevye represented the ultimate articulation of Jewish
life in all of its humor and tragedy. His other major characters all operated within the same sphere of *shtetl* life: Menachem Mendel, the tragic *luftmensh* who, after failing time
and again, finally abandons his long-suffering wife Sheinah-
Sheindel and flees to America; Mottel, the happy-go-lucky
orphan who joins his brother in illegal flight across the Russian border, and in a series of hilarious adventures journeys
to the Lower East Side of New York to make a new life for
himself, to make America his surrogate parent.

Nonetheless, Tevye is unique. The Tevye stories represent
a small fraction of Sholom Aleichem's *corpus*, which in some
editions runs to twenty-eight volumes, but not one of Sholom
Aleichem's other characters is placed at the crossroads of
history as Tevye is. He is the epitome of the *shtetl* patriarch,
a Hassidic follower, a semi-learned Jew who prays three
times a day and ironically thanks God for helping him starve
to death. His relationship with his Maker is personal, intimate, and most definitely one to one. Tevye understands the
Jew's purpose on earth: to suffer and to do God's will, but at
least to enjoy the luxury of being able to complain a bit. His
greatest pleasure is the rare time he finds for study. He loves
to quote the Talmud, which he knows with delightful imper-
fection. His misinterpretations and translations from the Hebrew are an inside joke between Sholom Aleichem and his
reader, as both chuckle with good humor at Tevye, the Jew
who would be a scholar. He is a philosopher, a humorist, but
above all, he is the head of the family, the Jewish patriarch,
a man who understands tradition and the meaning of the con-

tinuity implied in being a Jew. As such, Tevye has little time for and less interest in the outside world, the world of modernity. It is this attitude which produces tragedy for Tevye and his beloved Golde, his wife of many years.

The Tevye stories are family stories, familiar to all those Yiddish readers who almost exclusively comprised Sholom Aleichem's audience. He could count with relative certainty on his readers' understanding *shtetl* tradition; Sholom Aleichem was certain of both his and his readers' familiarity with the centuries-old values and heritage, and this certainty affected his writing. He had in Tevye a figure whose experiences paralleled those of the people who were reading about him. Tevye's family was the Jewish family of the Pale. When Tevye described himself as a *shlimmazel,* thousands of other luckless Jews could nod in sympathy.

Tevye considered himself a *shlimmazel* because God in His infinite wisdom had blessed him with all daughters! Among all Tevye's children there was no one to say the prayer for the dead parents, a privilege reserved (in this religion often described as sexist and worse) for males. But Tevye loves his daughters; he talks of their beauty and intelligence constantly. Sholom Aleichem gives Tevye ample opportunity to talk, because the stories are framed to provide the greatest possible exposure for his ideas and philosophy. Sholom Aleichem was fully aware of the literary giants writing in the Russian language, and he borrowed freely from Chekhov's monologues, joining the Russian literary tradition with the Yiddish one started by Mendele, who regularly appeared in his own narratives as a storyteller or listener. Sholom Aleichem is the audience in the Tevye stories, and it is to him that Tevye reveals his happiness and troubles. In the telling, Tevye also reveals the entire fabric of Jewish life in the Pale, familiar in every detail to the audience. The irony is supreme, because Tevye may not understand what he is revealing, although the Jewish reader comprehends the point which Sholom Aleichem, both inside and outside the narrative flow, is making. While avoiding the often crushing didacticism of Mendele, Sholom Aleichem still presses his point, that the *shtetl* world is coming to an end, and our children have other ideas.

Tevye Wins a Fortune (Dos Groyse Gevins)

So thoroughly was Sholom Aleichem inside the mind of his reader that he knew instinctively that first things still had to come first, and before tragedy could strike, there first had to be a satisfactory *parnosseh*. In the first of the Tevye stories, Sholom Aleichem provides us with a Jewish fairy tale. Tevye is not a dairyman; "with God's help, I starved to death," he informs Sholom Aleichem at the outset of the story, which finds him barely surviving as a hauler of wood whose only worldly possession is a wagon drawn by a broken-down horse. Tevye confronts his God with the same humanity, honest annoyance, and good humor which marks him even during his greatest travail: "All-powerful and All-merciful, great and good, kind and just, how does it happen that to some people you give everything and to others nothing?" [5] He has paused for a moment to say his morning prayers, and to let the Lord know that in spite of his misery he has not lost hope in Divine Will: "A Jew must always hope, must never lose hope. And in the meantime, what if we waste away to a shadow? For that we are Jews—the Chosen People, the envy and admiration of the world!"

The story he is telling Sholom Aleichem, however, is anything but tragic. While hauling his wood, Tevye came upon two Jewish women lost in the woods near Boiberik, the summer resort village where the Jewish *shayne*, the few wealthy, spend their vacation. Of course, not every Jew who went to Boiberik was rich. It was a sign of *yichus* if one went on summer vacation, for any length of time, and even the impoverished Jews made an effort at some time during the summer to leave the *shtetl* for a few days, to demonstrate their ability "to go to the mountains." In Boiberik one found elegant *dachas* as well as crowded *kochalayns,* boarding houses in which vacationers shared stove and kitchen table, "cooking alone," as the Yiddish word implies.

After some of his pleasant banter, Tevye volunteers to drive the women back to their *dacha,* where he is showered with pocket money by their grateful relatives. As he sweeps the money into his pockets, Tevye exclaims: "May God give you everything you desire ten times over! May you have all that is good, nothing but joy! And now good night and good luck, and God be with you!" As if by God's personal intervention, Tevye's life has been completely transformed. He was also promised a dried-up milk cow, and after a few brandies, the overjoyed and slightly tipsy drayman goes home to tell the good news to his wife and seven daughters.

The contrast between Tevye's high spirits and his wife Golde's bitterness is heightened when Golde thinks that her husband might be drunk. Again, the author was fully certain that his readers understood the background and experience of the Jewish woman of the *shtetl,* her frustrations and her anger. When Golde greets Tevye with a stream of curses and denunciations, it made perfectly good sense. Here was a *shtetl* wife, married for nearly twenty years, the result of an arrangement made by a matchmaker.[6] She has worked as hard as her husband, borne seven children, and in return had received very little reward. Unlike her husband, she did not have the solace of the Talmud or Jewish learning to support her. Her husband had not provided her with any status in the community, so she lacked any sign of measurable dignity, any *yichus* whatsoever. She had married a man of little standing, and their lives together had been filled with the typical *shtetl* frustrations which poverty inevitably produced. When Tevye walks happily into their hut, she explodes: "A black and endless Mazel-Tov to you. Why are you so happy, my beloved breadwinner, my goldspinner?!" As Tevye tells it: "She lets me have it, all the curses she knows, as only a woman can." But when Tevye places the thirty-seven rubles on the table and tells the story of the two women, the milk cow, and the reward, she breaks down, weeps and emerges a changed person. She becomes the wife of "Reb Tevye," a man of status, who takes the rubles, buys another cow, and becomes a dairyman.

As if by magic, Tevye and Golde are transformed into *shtetl* Jews with some modest *yichus*. Tevye's world is radically changed by the scraps of money given to him by the wealthy of Boiberik. The plot, however, is almost incidental. What is important—and also disturbing—in this first Tevye story is the picture which Sholom Aleichem paints of Jewish life in the Pale. The tragedy of the wretched majority in the *shtetl*, the fatalism with which the poor accept their misery, the almost naturalistic grimness of their deteriorating existence, all that turns around completely when a few rubles change the structure of Tevye's world. Sholom Aleichem does not want the point to be missed. This is a story, to be sure, with a happy ending, but the author does more than merely imply that the poor cannot just wait for happy endings. We are left with a picture of economic despair and general wretchedness which dominates *shtetl* life. Tevye seems temporarily spared; but nothing has changed the world around him.

The Bubble Bursts (A Boydem)

The framework of all the Tevye stories is the same. Tevye, by chance, meets Sholom Aleichem and relates to him the recent events of his life in the tiny village *shtetl* which he calls home, Anatevka, as well as in the near-by more urban *shtetl* of Kasrilevke (Sholom Aleichem's imaginary and archetypal Jewish townlet). In "The Bubble Bursts," [7] Tevye was relieved of the enormous economic burden of having to struggle for his family. He now sees himself able to provide suitable dowries for his seven daughters, Golde seems modestly satisfied with her new status in life, and Tevye has acquired a small amount of savings. But he reminds the reader and Sholom Aleichem of a Jewish saying known to all: *Yidishe ashires is vi shney in merts*—Jewish wealth is like snow in March. This is a story of wanting too much, of economic greed, and Sholom Aleichem is reminding his *shtetl* readers to be on guard against quick money and, above all, of the temptations associated with the Jewish *luftmensh*. Tevye has come to Yehupetz (the fictional equivalent of Kiev), for Tevye a city where he may come to buy goods or even sell his wares, but since it is not a legal place of residence for him, he cannot spend the night. Here he encounters the actual central figure of this episode, a character who occupies a place in Sholom Aleichem's works as prominent as Tevye: Menachem Mendel, a distant relative, illegally living in Yehupetz instead of his native Kasrilevke, where his wife Sheina-Sheindel weeps out of bitterness and humiliation at having such a failure for a husband.[8] He is, as Maurice Samuel once described him, "the apotheosis of Jewish rootlessness," the tragic entrepreneur-hustler willing to do or to sell anything for a profit, for whom the sunshine is always just around the corner. Hanging around in front of the Yehupetz stock exchange, Menachem Mendel lives in a world of shadows, looking over his shoulder for the police, in the midst of a windstorm of stock market quotations, commissions, futures, and dashed hopes. He is the eternal Jewish loser, but Tevye does not know this until he learns from bitter experience. After friendly introductions and family greetings, Tevye is convinced that the way to increase his money is to invest it with Menachem Mendel. After all, he is *mishpoche,* family, and can be trusted. Tevye dreams of becoming a benefactor and *nogid,* of building a new synagogue perhaps, and improving the ritual bathhouse.

Menachem Mendel seems to Tevye to possess the perfect combination of piety and business sense: "With God's help, the money will come pouring in."

The money does not come pouring in, and after some weeks Tevye returns to Yehupetz to look for his second cousin, once removed. He wanders into the stock exchange street and encounters a scene of bedlam:

> I can barely push my way through. People are running around like crazy, shouting, waving their hands, quarreling. I hear shouts of "*Putilov,* shares, stocks . . . he gave me his word . . . buy on margin . . . he owes me a fee . . . spit in his face . . ." I mutter to myself: "Get out, Tevye, before you get knocked down." God is our Father, Tevye the Dairyman is a sinner, Yehupetz is a city, and Menachem Mendel is a breadwinner. So this is where people make fortunes? So this is how they do their business? May God have mercy on you, Tevye, and on such business.

Suddenly, reflected in a window, Tevye sees his missing partner: "May our worst enemies look the way Menachem Mendel looked! A corpse laid out for burial looks cheerful by comparison." The poor wretch tells Tevye of his lost chances, of Tevye's lost money. At first, Tevye is furious: "For such a deed, for what you have done to me, you deserve to be stretched out right here in the middle of Yehupetz and flogged. . . . How can I face my wife, my children? Tell me, you robber, you murderer, you—the fires of *Gehenna,* the tortures of hell are too good for you." But after the therapeutic outburst, Tevye's humanity and compassion win out: "I look at him standing there, the poor *shlimmazel,* leaning against the wall, his head bent, his hat awry. He sighs and he groans and my heart turns over with pity."

As he contemplates his brief career as a near-*nogid,* Tevye's philosophical-religious foundation gives him ample support. He admits that he longed to be a rich man, but God felt that it was more important that Tevye should stay as he was: " 'You, Tevye', says God, 'stick to your cheese and butter and forget your dreams.' But what about hope? Naturally, the harder life is, the more you must hope. The poorer you are the more cheerful you must be."

In the first of the Tevye stories, Sholom Aleichem provides a satisfactory economic basis on which to operate. He shows Tevye as wretchedly poor, then suitably arranges for his economic salvation and security, with a measure of adequate *yichus*. The family remains primarily in the background, although his total reason for existence is presented against this background. In the second story, Sholom Aleichem demonstrates the dangers of too much success for the Jew and the potential hazards of being involved in the marginal existence of a Menachem Mendel, who is really the center of the narrative and the tragic pivot around which Tevye for a brief moment rotates. Sholom Aleichem is preparing the reader for Tevye's ultimate crises, which concern the family directly; and by family Sholom Aleichem clearly understood what was meant: children. Menachem Mendel's tragic life serves as a prelude, as an example of the unnatural life of such a creature, living away from wife and children. Tevye urges him to return to Kasrilevke, to his wife grown bitter with increasing loneliness: " 'Don't remind me that,' he says with a deep sigh. 'I get enough from her as it is, both hot and cold. If you could see the letters she writes me you would admit that I am a saint to put up with it. But that's a small matter. That's what a wife is for—to bury her husband alive. There are worse things than that. I have also, as you know, a mother-in-law. I don't have to go into detail. You have met her.' "

Modern Children (Hayntike Kinder) [9]

When Sholom Aleichem focuses on Tevye's conflicts with his daughters, he consciously exposes the fundamental generational conflict at the heart of the break-up of the *shtetl* world. He heightens the conflict by making all of Tevye's children female, the sex most identified with traditions, adherence to the old ways, generally lacking the educational advantage which might permit a young person to acquire ideas perhaps not found in the *shtetl* environment. There are five children who are central characters of the Tevye stories: Tzeitel, Hodel, Chava, Shprintze, and Beilke. Each one is brought into conflict with Tevye, and he responds characteristically in each instance, depending on the seriousness of the situation. In each successive story, Sholom Aleichem increases the tension, raises the cost in emotion and alienation for Tevye as he faces the mysteries of parenthood in a world which he thought he understood, but which is rapidly drawing away from him. The tragedy for Tevye, and the world that he represents, is that he never comes to understand what has happened. All of his Jewish education and values have not prepared him to deal with his daughters' increasing awareness of the outside world. On close examination, it becomes apparent, however, that within Tevye's frame of reference, he should not have had to understand any more than he does. He has not changed: his children have. His Judaism simply had not supplied him with any particular measure of parental insight.

In "Modern Children" the tragedy is avoided, ironically, by Tevye's own humanity and understanding. He has daughters to marry off, a serious enough problem in *shtetl* life. In terms of communal ethos, as we have seen, an unmarried daughter is an embarrassment to the family, a "shame." Old maids were looked upon as unnatural. This must be understood when Tevye hears that the widowed butcher Lazer Wolf is interested in his oldest daughter, the beautiful Tzeitel. In spite of the disaster with Menachem Mendel, Tevye is still a person of some eminence in the community. "And besides, with God's help, I'm not the same Tevye I used to be. Now the best match, even in Yehupetz, is not beyond my reach."

Tevye has talked himself into accepting Lazer Wolf as a son-in-law, even if the butcher brings some drawbacks to the match:

> He has children as old as she was. But then I reminded myself: what a lucky thing for her. She'll have everything she wants. And if he is not so good looking? There are other things besides looks. There was only one thing I really had against him: he could barely read his prayers. But, then, could everyone be a scholar? There are plenty of wealthy men who don't know one letter from another. Just the same, if it's their luck to have a little money they get all the respect and honor a man could want.

Respect and honor—*yichus* and *koved*. Sholom Aleichem, through Tevye, speaks a language so thoroughly understood in terms of *shtetl* mores that a mere two words conjure up a system's entire social structure. For the reader, as well as for Tevye, the problem of Lazer Wolf's age or of his lack of learning are easily overcome. He has sufficient *yichus;* this is a match which will bring honor to Tevye's family. The two older men, however, ironically take a step which suggests that they, too, are somewhat active participants in the passing of the old ways. Lazer Wolf says to Tevye: "You know, Reb Tevye, that I have been a widower for quite a while now. So I thought, why do I have to go looking all over the world, get mixed up with matchmakers, those sons of Satan?" There is no *shadchan,* no traditional matchmaker to make the arrangements.

Tevye then hints at still another deviation which is unacceptable even to Lazer Wolf. Here the flaw is not in the changing values of the *shtetl;* it is within Tevye's personality, his gentle nature. After the marriage has been agreed to between the men, Tevye mentions: "Besides, there's Tzeitel herself to be asked," to which the astonished butcher replies: "What foolishness! Is this something to ask about? *Tell* her,

Reb Tevye. Go home, tell her what is what, and get the wedding canopy ready!" Lazer Wolf's attitude is perfectly consistent with *shtetl* traditions. Tevye reluctantly sees matters that way as well, and returns home to inform Golde of the betrothal. Her response is consistent with Lazer Wolf's: to get busy with the dowry and preparations for the wedding.

But Tzeitel, when she eventually discovers that she is to be married to the widower, tearfully confronts her father on the road and begs him to call off the wedding. It is at this point that Tevye's nature gets in the way of tradition. Although Tevye prides himself on being the strong male figure, "never crying like a woman, not Tevye," he relents. He never asked her if she wanted to marry Lazer Wolf, yet he cannot turn her down when she pleads for his help. Before giving in, however, Tevye reaches into his *shtetl* bag of tricks for one more try. He instinctively grasps the nature of parent-child relationships built up over centuries, the strong sense of familial obligation and shared responsibilities. He counts on this when he appeals to Tzeitel's sense of guilt; a psychological weapon always at the disposal of the *shtetl* parent who has inculcated an enormous expression of honor, respect, obedience, and unity into his or her children: "So it was not meant that we should have a little joy in our old age, after all our hard work, harnessed, you might say, day and night to a wheelbarrow. No happiness. Only poverty and misery and bad luck over and over. . . ." But Tzeitel's tears overflow, and Tevye capitulates.

Now he has an even bigger problem: how to tell Golde. Yet even before he can address this dilemma his *tzurus,* his aggravations, are compounded when the tailor Mottel Kamzoil appears before Tevye as a matchmaker. Tevye listens calmly, until he discovers that the match Mottel is proposing is between Tzeitel—and himself. "When he said that I jumped up from the ground as if I had been scalded, and he jumped too, and there we were, facing each other like bristling roosters.

'Either you're crazy,' I said to him, 'or simply out of your mind! What are you, everything? The matchmaker, the bridegroom, the ushers all rolled into one? I suppose you'll play the wedding march too! I never heard of such a thing—arranging a match for oneself!' " Then Tevye discovers that the young people have been seeing each other for over a year without his knowledge. He is shocked on two accounts; first, from the hurt he suffers as the head of the family who had been ignorant of events; secondly, in terms of *yichus*: "How does a tailor like Mottel fit into the picture as my son-in-law?" Later, when Golde is finally told of the state of things, she cries out, "A *tailor!* Where does a tailor come into our family?!" In terms of village status, Mottel's occupation is very near the bottom. In dealing with Mottel and Tzeitel, Tevye now finds himself totally disoriented. He does not know what to do, his traditions have been violated: "Do I still have the right to ask him something about my daughter, or doesn't anyone have to ask a father anymore?" Tevye is puzzled and hurt. "What did they mean—pledging their troth? What kind of world has this become? A boy meets a girl and says to her, 'Let us pledge our troth'. Why, it's just too free and easy, that's all!" Tevye is unable to act as his forefathers might have, namely driving Mottel out of the village with a cane and bringing charges against him before the rabbi. Instead, he sighs and tries to figure a way to cope with the *real* problem, his wife.

Here, Tevye is on surer ground. He understands his mate and contemporary. He never thinks of telling her the truth. In Tevye's world, the woman is dealt with through superstition, through the innate weakness of her education and upbringing. Tevye resorts to superstition to inform her that her daughter is to be married to the impoverished tailor Mottel Kamzoil. He awakens from an apparent nightmare to gasp out that he has received a visitation from Golde's grandmother and then later from Lazer Wolf's first wife, urging

Tevye first to break the engagement with the butcher and then to have his daughter betrothed to the tailor Mottel Kamzoil. For a split second Golde recovers from her terror to complain about Mottel's profession, but the nightmare—or at least Tevye's account of it—convinces her.

The problems are solved, the ending is happy. Mottel marries Tzeitel and they settle down to *shtetl* life, living in poverty but joining Tevye and Golde in the traditional Jewish extended family, first two, later three generations sharing life with one another. Even if children have moved to another neighboring cottage hut, they join their parents completely in the experience of Jewish family life.

However, the reader has seen what Tevye has not. Tevye's world had been challenged, and in the challenge changes had taken place which Tevye in his frame of reference cannot comprehend. Tzeitel has married for love. Sholom Aleichem permits Tevye a closing complaint: "So go complain about modern children. You slave for them, do everything for them! And they tell you that they know better. And . . . maybe they do. . . ." This is Sholom Aleichem's style of criticism; it is gentle, ironic, infinitely more subtle than Mendele's aggressive didacticism and morality. Sholom Aleichem is preparing the reader, through Tevye's experiences, for the spiritual and ideological conflicts which he saw as inevitable in the old Jewish world of the Pale. He gives this story the luxury of a happy ending. It was, for Tevye, the last happiness he was to know.

Hodel [10]

With "Hodel" Sholom Aleichem demonstrates the tragic impact of contemporary events on the traditional life of Tevye's *shtetl*. The target is most clearly the family; for Sholom Aleichem it is an opportunity to show what centuries of unchanging attitudes have produced in Jewish life in the Pale. In Tevye's conflict with his daughter the reader encounters a Jewish father who simply is incapable of communication with his children, or, for that matter, with his wife. The generation conflict is at the core of Tevye's family tragedy.

Sholom Aleichem uses a sharp sense of dramatic irony in underlining the alienation of Tevye from the events which ultimately control his life. At the beginning of the narrative he boasts of Hodel's prowess: "She can write and read—Yiddish and Russian both. And books—she swallows like dumplings. You may be wondering how a daughter of Tevye happens to be reading books, while her father deals in butter and cheese. That's what I'd like to know myself. . . ." While Tevye shines with pride in his daughter, the reader is alerted, because the *shtetl* reader's instincts have made him aware of the problems which a too highly educated daughter might bring. Not only was education for the female undesirable because it allegedly wasted knowledge, it also made it difficult to make a proper match. Who, after all, wanted a wife who possessed more knowledge than the husband? This was an integral part of the *shtetl* value system and Sholom Aleichem's audience would immediately grasp its implications. Tevye's pride in his daughter would therefore not meet with the same enthusiastic response in Sholom Aleichem's audience, and their anxiety would prove justifiable.

Hodel does indeed transcend the available youth of the *shtetl*, but, ironically, it is Tevye himself who unwittingly provides the suitable young man for his daughter. While driving the roads near his village he picks up young Pertschik, the son of a local impoverished cigarette maker. Pertschik is one of the handful of daring youths who probed the outside world. He left the *shtetl* to attempt to break the quota system at the university. He has studied, starved, and become a radical socialist. Tevye, isolated in his world, cut off from the forces around him, does not understand the drives which move Pertschik to violence:

> There was only one thing I didn't like about him, and that was the way he had of suddenly disappearing. . . . He had the wildest notions, the most peculiar ideas. Everything was upside down, topsy-turvy. For instance, according to his way of thinking, a poor man was far more important than a rich one, and if he happened to be a worker, then he was really the brightest jewel in the diadem! He who toiled with his hands stood first in his estimation.

The realities of the world beyond him have not penetrated Tevye's protective tradition. He invites Pertschik to help tutor his daughters, not realizing the impact the new ideology will have on the receptive Hodel. Tevye is unwittingly helping to destroy his own world. The inevitable occurs, and Pertschik and Hodel announce their betrothal "in the modern fashion" to Tevye, simply by telling him that they plan to marry; furthermore, immediately after the ceremony, Pertschik will have to go away. Tevye takes the news with his usual mixture of wit and pathos: "When was the contract signed? And why didn't you invite me to the ceremony? Don't you think I have the slightest interest in the matter? I joke with them, and yet my heart is breaking." There is no traditional wedding, no celebration, no *naches* for Tevye. As for Golde, again no one even bothers to tell her the truth, neither Hodel nor Tevye: "She kept plaguing me: what were they in such a hurry about? Go try to explain their haste to a woman. But don't worry—I invented a story, 'great, powerful, and marvelous,' as the Bible says, about a rich aunt in Yehupetz, an inheritance, all sorts of foolishness." Sholom Aleichem calls into question once again the fundamental structure of the Jewish family in *shtetl* life at this moment of dramatic transition to the modern world. What worked in the past simply does not work in the present. The husband does not communicate with the wife; nor do the children communicate with either parent.

Meanwhile, Tevye still does not understand the nature of Pertschik's activity, nor does Hodel bother to explain. He suggests that perhaps the young husband has fallen in with a band of thieves, and Hodel bursts out laughing. The laughter turns bitter, however, when Hodel has to tell her father that Pertschik has been arrested and sent to jail in Siberian exile, and that she must join him. Here we are faced with a tragedy whose implications can only be understood in terms of the *shtetl* family. We have two married daughters, no grandchildren as yet, and now a daughter, a child actually moving out of the *shtetl*. There is nothing that Tevye can recognize as normal in these events; they are, in fact, cataclysmic. The loss of a child, her physical removal, even voluntarily, from the village environment, is an event that signals the greatest possible misfortune. Even when he takes Hodel to the train station and they finally weep together, Tevye never understands what it is that Pertschik has done. Hodel makes a desperate effort to communicate with her father: "He was a man, she insisted, who cared nothing about himself. Everything he did was for humanity at large, especially for those who toiled with their hands—that is, the workers. That made no sense to me."

None of this makes sense to Tevye. The generation conflict, for all the use and misuse of the term, is never more graphically treated than in this story of a daughter's transcendence of her parents' world. Hodel has moved up and beyond Tevye's frame of reference, out of his religious and *shtetl* sphere, into a secular one in which the issues are less man's relationship to God than man's relationship to man. The *shtetl* traditions have not prepared Tevye for this. Without her father's knowledge, Hodel has become embroiled in the problems of modern Russia and modern society. Tevye's pride has turned to pain, but it is pain without understanding.

Chava[11]

There can be little doubt that Sholom Aleichem intended this to be the last of the Tevye stories. Tragedy reaches its ultimate level for the Jewish family in the *shtetl*: nothing can go beyond the injury associated with the child who marries outside of Judaism. But Sholom Aleichem is not merely concerned with presenting a story with obvious sentimental-pathetic implications for the Jew. That would be easy enough, knowing the range of tragic events which would be guaranteed to stir the hearts of the *shtetl* inhabitants. Instead, he clearly wishes to demonstrate that, even with this horrendous event, the full implications of which are shared by all the readers, there remains a problem of generation and communication at the center of the conflict. Sholom Aleichem manages to put even this problem in the form of a struggle between two worlds, one as it disintegrates, the other as it comes into being.

When Tevye sees Chava talking to the Gentile town clerk Fyedka, he is concerned. He asks his daughter:

> " 'What was Fyedka doing here?' 'Nothing,' she said. 'What do you mean, nothing?' 'We were just talking.' 'What business do you have talking with Fyedka?' I asked. 'We've known each other for a long time,' she said. 'Congratulations! A fine friend you've picked for yourself!' "

Chava's perception of Fyedka is not one shared by Tevye. For him, Fyedka is no more than a *goy*, a stereotype built up by centuries of pogroms, threats, and fear: "I don't know who he is. I've never seen his family tree. But I am sure he must be descended from a long and honorable line. His father must have been a shepherd or a janitor, or else just a plain drunkard." The exchange between father and daughter goes to the core of the alienation: " 'Who his father was I don't know and I don't care to know. But Fyedka himself is not an ordinary person. I would tell you, but you wouldn't understand. Fyedka is a second Gorky.' 'A second Gorky? And who, may I ask, was the first Gorky?' 'Gorky,' she said, 'is one of the greatest men living in the world today.' 'Where does he live,' I asked, 'this sage of yours, what is his occupation and what words of wisdom has he spoken?' " The hopelessness of attempting any communication between these two worlds becomes apparent. Once again, the revolution has come to Tevye's world, and he is uncomprehending. His children do not look to a world of *yichus*, of parents' occupations and status in the community. They look to Gorky, to the world of his play *The Lower Depths*, and to a humanitarian revolution that will finally transcend religious sectarianism. In none of the other Tevye stories is the patriarch made to look as narrow-minded when faced with modernism as in this one. Even the priest seems to have more tolerance than Tevye: "Your child is reaching out for a different world, and you don't understand her, or else you don't wish to understand her." Tevye seems to be concerned only with his own image in the community, and the unbearable loss of face that is involved when a child marries a non-Jew. He repeats like a litany: "The pain is great, but the disgrace—the disgrace is even greater." This is the leit-motif which Sholom Aleichem chooses to characterize Tevye's attitude. Tevye's shame preoccupies him; he loses his perspective as a father because his status is threatened by his daughter's marriage to a *goy*.

But Sholom Aleichem's implied criticism of Tevye can only go so far. When it comes down to the crunch, he still must side with the Jew, simply because Tevye the father is unable to regain his lost daughter, even if he tries to. Tevye wishes to speak to Chava, but is informed by the priest that this will be impossible. "She is now under my protection." In this way Sholom Aleichem demonstrates the frustration and futility of the Jew in Czarist Russia. There is no recourse for Tevye. He cannot speak to his daughter, cannot approach her. She is now officially a ward of the state, and the Jew's access to his own child is denied him. The point strikes home hard, and Chava's decision to seek refuge with the priest transcends her intellectual prowess, her humanitarianism, indeed, her entire advantage. She has betrayed her family, abandoned her parents, and in spite of Tevye's apparent narrow-mindedness, she emerges as the main contributor to the family disruption. Even when she encounters her father on the road and begs for recognition, to Tevye she is dead, no longer a member of the Jewish community. Tevye has rent his garments and said the prayer for the dead for the daughter he has lost. He will not speak to her, will no longer acknowledge her existence.

"Chava" has all the ingredients of Jewish soap opera, or, for that matter, any ethnic minority melodrama, particularly in terms of the older generation. There could be no greater calamity, no greater loss of face than that signaled by an intermarriage, the merging, in this case, of Jew and Gentile. Conversion meant nothing, was not accepted in *shtetl* terms. Fyedka would always be the *goy,* the *shaygits* (Gentile boy), even if he were to accept Judaism. Sholom Aleichem's treatment of the theme is intended to underline the tragedy on both sides, not just for the parents. Indeed, he focuses on the *shtetl's* inability, that is, Tevye's inability, to deal with the invasion of ideas which he considers either foreign or threatening. The Jewish family succumbs to the tragedy of events which it has not been prepared to deal with.

At the end, Tevye bids goodbye to Sholom Aleichem. The final curtain has come down on Tevye's world. Where does the dairyman encounter greater loss than this, greater shame and bereavement? The conclusion of the story makes it clear that this is the end of Tevye the *shlimmazel*: "And if you should write, write about something else, not about me. Forget about me—no more Tevye the Dairyman!" Tevye's action is automatic in terms of Jewish tradition and law: he must drive his daughter from the family. Yet he seems to understand that at this point in history Chava's defection is more

than the loss of a child—it is the loss of his world. Tevye is beyond forgiveness; he could not, even with the humanity he
possesses, excuse Chava's act. Sholom Aleichem, by framing
her action with the crush of events produced by changing
times, underlines the tragedy which no doubt will be repeated in thousands of *shtetl* families in the ghettoes in the
East and eventually under the shadow of the Delancey Street
Bridge in New York as well. For Tevye, the Jewish Everyman,
is helpless, and cannot gain strength from his traditions. They
have told him only to resist and to struggle against those
forces trying to destroy his and his fathers' world.

Shprintze[12]

For Sholom Aleichem, the remaining Tevye stories were an
afterthought. It was difficult for the author to find a theme
more striking that that of apostasy, and one notices the
strained thematic expression in this story of rich Jew against
poor Jew, of *shayne Yidn* and *proste Yidn,* which ends in the
utterly melodramatic and highly questionable suicide of a rejected Jewish girl, in this case Tevye's daughter Shprintze.
But in terms of the sociology of the *shtetl* and our understanding of the problems which were confronting the Jew at
this decisive moment, the story is a historical document of
considerable interest. Even the overromanticized aspects are
helpful in our understanding of the social tensions of the
shtetl in disintegration. Once again, the family is pivotal;
once again, Tevye's own inability to perceive his children's
world causes his own personal tragedy. This is a story of
yichus, but it is also one of a definite historical epoch that
provides us with additional information concerning the Jews'
plight in Czarist Russia. Tevye greets Sholom Aleichem with
"It's a score of years since we have seen each other.... We
have lived through Kishinev and a Constitution, through po-

groms and disasters of every kind." Sholom Aleichem had not written a Tevye story for nearly ten years, not the twenty which Tevye alleges in his greeting. The times have indeed changed. In the post-1905 period, the exuberance and revolutionary fervor of Hodel and Chava has given way to a new spirit, to one of resignation and dismay. The hopes of those early revolutionaries were dashed by the crushing of the popular uprisings. As for the Jews, Russia's humiliation at the hands of the Japanese in the Russo-Japanese War left the Czarist government looking for a scapegoat, and the Jews were all too convenient. The horrible pogroms in Kishinev and Bessarabia cost nearly twenty thousand lives. Meanwhile, over one million Jews had already abandoned their homes and had fled to North or South America. Sholom Aleichem saw the occurrence of what he might have predicted a decade earlier; the *shtetl* world was indeed falling apart.

So it is not surprising that Sholom Aleichem now turns to themes connected specifically with this post-turn-of-the-century generation, and uses Tevye and his family to underline these themes. Sholom Aleichem abandons the *shtetl* environment for the city, for the Jewish world no longer pivots on village life. But Sholom Aleichem never accepted the city as an alternative to *shtetl* existence; he acknowledged that the old ways would disappear, but he would not concede that all aspects of the new life were going to represent an improvement for Jews. Sholom Aleichem saw the city as a place fraught with danger for Jews, for the Menachem Mendels who lost themselves in the dark shadows. Most of all he objected to the *nouveau riche* Jews who left behind in the *shtetls* any sense of Jewish ethics which they might have possessed. They represent the worst aspects of assimilation, materialism, and shallowness. Like Saul Bellow's New York, Sholom Aleichem's Yehupetz provides an atmosphere which fosters a kind of Jewish isolation from the taproots of tradition.

During the summer Tevye finds many new customers, vacationers who spend a few weeks in Boiberik and the surrounding *shtetls*. One of them is a rich widow who has a spoiled, wild son, Aarontchik, who passes his days fishing and rides horses on the Sabbath, while he waits for the end of vacation and the return to the city. Tevye, arrogant in spite of all his tragedies, admonishes the widow for not disciplining the lad: "I was honestly sorry for the mother. She wept and wailed and asked me what she should do. She begged me to have a talk with him." Tevye points out that such a woman would not be permitted to remain a widow in the *shtetl*, that it was considered improper for a woman to attempt to bring up a boy without some male discipline. The young man, instead of throwing Tevye out of his house, laughs at the presumptuous butter and egg man, and they become friends. Tevye invites Aarontchik to his house, where the inevitable happens: he falls in love with one of Tevye's daughters, Shprintze. Even if Tevye was imprudent enough to allow the young people to see each other, at first he realizes that all the rules of both *shtetl* and city etiquette make such a match impossible. The family *yichus* of the widow would not tolerate her son marrying a dairyman's daughter, and Tevye is quick to point this out when Aarontchik says he plans to marry Shprintze: " 'Every cantor sings according to his ability and every orator speaks of what concerns him. If you want to know what kind of orator you are, talk it over with your mother. She will put you straight.' " When the young man says his mother's permission is not necessary, Tevye bursts out: " 'Of course you have to tell your mother, and of course she will tell you that you are an imbecile, and what's more, she will be right.' " Tevye understands the rules of *yichus*, he is fully aware that he has no right to hope for a marriage with such a wealthy family as Aarontchik's. " 'Certainly she will be right. What sort of bridegroom would you make my

Shprintze? And what kind of match is she for you? And most important of all, what kind of relative-by-marriage will I be to your mother?' " *Most important of all,* says Tevye. Nevertheless he permits himself the luxury of a little fantasy, and dreams of his daughter marrying a millionaire. Finally the young man prevails, saying that he is over eighteen and able to make up his own mind. Tevye has visions of grandeur once again.

But Aarontchik suddenly disappears, and Tevye receives an urgent message that the widow must speak to him at her home in Boiberik. The unsuspecting Tevye sets off happily for a visit with his prospective relative by marriage, only to encounter someone else: " 'I sent for you', said a short, round barrel of a man, with a sparse little beard and a heavy gold chain around his stomach. 'I am the widow's brother, Aarontchik's uncle. . . . I want you to tell me, but tell me frankly, how much it will cost us all told. . . . I am asking how much this affair will cost us.' " Tevye then has to listen to a stream of abuse about the nerve of a dairyman who would dare to marry his daughter into such a prominent family. The final humiliation for Tevye is the offer of a bribe to break the engagement.

For once in his life, Tevye is struck dumb. He simply leaves the presence of this obnoxious *nogid,* who possesses the characteristics which Sholom Aleichem obviously associates with wealth: the large stomach encircled by a gold chain. The impact on Shprintze is devastating, and she takes the very un-Jewish step of drowning herself, a deed acceptable only within the frame of reference of Jewish romance. For the first time in the Tevye stories we find a lack of that spiritual element which permeated the world of the *shtetl.* What we now encounter is the material society which in no way pleases Sholom Aleichem, and which places little value on what either Tevye or the shtetl have to offer.

81

Tevye Goes to Palestine (Tevye fort keyn Erets-Isroel) [13]

This is once again a story of the Constitutional period of 1904–05, the daughter is Beilke, and she more than anyone else understands what has happened to her family during the past decade. " 'Don't compare me to Hodel! Hodel lived in her time, and I live in mine!' " she says when her father complains about her lack of attention. The times, the environment around Tevye, everything has altered dramatically. Golde is dead, a victim of change. She proved to be less adaptable than Tevye, and could not exist without her family around her. Golde remained faithful to the old, familiar role of the *shtetl* wife and mother:

> She couldn't bear it any longer, seeing them scatter and disappear the way they did, some one way, some another. "Heavens above!" she used to say, "what have I left to live for, all alone without kith or kin? Why, even a cow is lonesome when you wean her calf away from her." That's the way she spoke, and she wept bitterly.

Golde provides us with an exceptional view of the tragedy of change. The sole purpose of existence is the family, her exclusive function to act as mother, and later, grandmother. With her children gone, with no apparent interest in perpetuating the family structure, she gives in to her despair and dies.

Tevye is left alone to face the very uncertain future. His daughter Beilke has been married to a wealthy young man from Yehupetz, and we are not impressed by the description which Ephraim the Matchmaker gives when he approaches Tevye: " 'He is a contractor, this Padhatzur, he builds houses and factories and bridges. He was in Japan during the war and made a fortune. He rides in a carriage drawn by fiery steeds, he has a lackey at the door, a bathtub right in his own house, furniture from Paris, and a diamond ring on his finger. . . . And he's looking for a pretty girl; it makes no difference who she is. . . .' " They were married, and honeymooned, as Tevye says, "in Nitaly somewhere," and have settled amidst the splendor of Padhatzur's recently acquired wealth.

What is this Jew? He knows nothing of Talmud or Torah, is ignorant of even the most rudimentary ethics of Judaism, and apparently made his wealth as a war profiteer while living in the enemy homeland. Tevye is called to visit his son-in-law, sees the show of riches, and describes the world of the *nouveau riche*:

> He talks enough for two. His mouth doesn't shut for a moment. In all my life I have never seen a man who could jabber so endlessly and say so little, interspersing all of his talk with that sniggering laugh of his. . . . Besides us three, there was another guest at the table—a fellow with bulging cheeks. I don't know who or what he was, but he seemed to be a glutton of no mean proportions. All the time Padhatzur was talking and laughing, he went on stuffing himself. . . . This one guzzled and the other one talked. . . . It was all about contracts, government pronouncements, banks, money, Japan.

Beilke merely sits silently by, a representative of the world she had earlier described: "Hodel grew up in a time when the whole world rocked on its foundations, when it was ready at any moment to turn upside down. In those days people were concerned about the world and forgot about themselves. Now that the world is back to where it was, people think about themselves and forget about the world." The idealists are gone, even those who possessed the fortitude to leave have pulled up stakes. What remains are those Jews either caught between the end of the old and the creation of the new, the generation of Tevye, or the profiteers, the morally degenerate whom Sholom Aleichem considers the parasites of the Jewish world, with values in no way related to either the old world's tradition or the new world's hopes. They unified the worst qualities of both worlds, and this is what Padhatzur coldly represents:

> Now that he was rich he wanted the honor of entertaining important people in his home, and to that end he was pouring out thousands of rubles, handing out charity in all directions. But money, it seems, isn't everything. You have to have family and background as well. He was willing to go to any length to prove that he wasn't a nobody, he boasted that he was descended from the great Padhatzurs, that his father was a celebrated contractor, too. "Though he knows," Beilke said, "quite well, and he knows that I know that his father was only a poor fiddler. And on top of that he keeps telling everyone that his wife's father is a millionaire."

Tevye has become a stranger in his own homeland, a very special kind of *luftmensh,* unable to find comfort or identity either in the past or in the future. Padhatzur wants him out of the picture, because Tevye's presence is an embarrassment to him. He urges Tevye either to go to America, or perhaps to Palestine. "Old Jews are always eager to go to Palestine." Padhatzur also agrees to arrange for Hodel and Pertschik's freedom, if they, too, will leave Russia—he wishes to be completely free of his *mishpoche.*

The evolution of family within the traditions of the *shtetl* reaches its old world culmination in this narrative. The idea of *mishpoche,* once the absolute foundation of social meaning and purpose, has become superfluous, replaced by an imaginary, reconstructed ideal more suitable to the upward mobility of those left behind. *Yichus* has become the only important value carried over from the past, and *yichus* without the moral framework of Torah is empty. Padhatzur, as he admits, would not recognize Torah if he saw it. This, then, represents the product of Jewish success in the outside world, the results of a kind of assimilation which Sholom

Aleichem certainly considers the result of the breakdown of the *shtetl* world.

Yet Sholom Aleichem's position is not a reactionary or cautious one. He does not advocate the return to *shtetl* values. One of his primary points throughout the Tevye stories has been the inability of that *shtetl* to move into the twentieth century. More detached, more removed than most of the Yiddish writers of his age, Sholom Aleichem was an observer of the tragedy which was acted out in the hundreds of *shtetls* of the Pale in the confrontation of generations. The inimical, almost Hegelian clash of these generational forces produced enormous changes, and resulted ultimately in the flowering of Yiddish culture in America. The great *Haskalah* that Sholom Aleichem had hoped for, the great Enlightenment could not occur in Czarist Russia. Only the Padhatzurs who were willing to forego their Judaism could succeed there. Tevye had to be left behind as well. The *shtetl* world, however, proved to be remarkably mobile, even transplantable. It found new roots on the Lower East Side of New York; and the *mishpoche*, the Jewish family, was once again the center of attention of Yiddish fiction. Indeed, Sholom Aleichem accompanied hundreds of thousands of these families, following his subject matter to the new homeland. As he lay dying, he was working on the story of Mottel, a Jewish child who had accompanied his brother and mother to the new world, and whose eyes were opening to the miracle of life in New York City. Had he not died, Sholom Aleichem no doubt would have become the chronicler of an even more difficult chapter for the Jewish family, as it now confronted a threat even greater than those of Czarist Russia and of modern ideas encroaching on the *shtetl*. In America there was freedom, no *shtetl* walls to hold the children in, and the challenge to the Jewish family was to become the major theme of Jewish literature both in Yiddish and in English.

5

A Sociology of Mishpoche Stereotypes

THE Tevye stories expose the specific dynamics of one Jewish family's struggle with tradition and the forces attempting to break away from it. What is revealed shows us the very special fabric of a *shtetl* family's relationships against the background of centuries of ingrained attitudes, expectations, and customs. But Tevye is not the sum total of Sholom Aleichem's work, and Sholom Aleichem is not the sum total of Yiddish literature. Nonetheless, if this literature can be said to have a *subject,* a unifying focus, it would be the family. We cannot possibly exhaust the theme of the Jewish family in Yiddish literature within a study of this scope, but it might be reasonable to expect at least an over-view of the literary types which this literature produced in dealing with the subject.

Sholom Aleichem, as the ultimate Yiddish writer of the *shtetl* world, was more intensely concerned with family life than any other Yiddish writer. In Golde and Tevye, he created a *shtetl* married couple that represented one of the more familiar patterns of relationships. There were others which did not involve self-assured patriarchs such as Tevye. Given the entire tradition of *shtetl* values, it would seem that the Golde-Tevye relationship could be accepted as the norm. The husband with certain *rights* of authority was complemented by the wife who also enjoyed privilege, but of a different kind, and very particularly of a kind not associated with learning and therefore inferior. But Sholom Aleichem also shows us situations which in *shtetl* terms he and his readers would have to judge "abnormal," in which the female has assumed the male prerogatives. In "The Purim Feast" and "Gymnasia" the central theme is the dominating wife, and the conception is sufficiently negative to make it clear that *shtetl* mores did not take kindly to this type of woman.

The form of "The Purim Feast" is particularly interesting. The narrator is an adult, although the story appears in a 1921 volume which Sholom Aleichem entitled *Mayses far yidishe kinder* ("Stories for Jewish Children"—this has never been translated into English). It would be more accurate to describe these brief narratives as stories *about* Jewish children, because it is the children against whom the action and events play. The young man (or is he old?) recalls the Purim celebration which took place annually at the home of his mother's brother, the *nogid* Uncle Hertz:

> "Look at that pair of hands!" And she slapped me smartly across my wrists to make me drop them. "When you sit at Uncle Hertz's table remember to keep your hands down, do you hear? And don't let your face get as red as Yadwocha the peasant girl's. And don't roll your eyes like a tomcat. Do you hear what I'm telling you? And sit up like a human being. And the main thing—is your nose. Oh that nose of yours! Come here and let me put that nose in order!"

The mother totally dominates the family, having received her authority from the *yichus* of her brother. Her husband is a weak *shlemihl* who stands by while the mother physically abuses his son. Whenever he attempts to assert even some modest authority, she verbally assaults him until he retreats. The most innocent remark by the father can be the prelude to an assault:

> I happened to be by one day when my father let something fall. Do you think it was something disrespectful? Not at

all. He only remarked to my mother: "Well, what's the news? Has your Hertz arrived yet, or not?" And she gave him such a fare-thee-well that my poor father didn't know whether to stand up or sit down. "What do you mean by my Hertz? What kind of talk is that? What sort of expression? What do you mean he is mine?" "Whose is he if not yours," said my father, trying to give battle. But he didn't advance far. My mother attacked him on all sides at once. "Well, if he is mine, what of it? You don't like it? His ancestry isn't good enough for you? You had to divide your father's inheritance with him? You never got any favors from him? Is that it?" "Who says I didn't," my father offered in a milder tone, ready to surrender himself. But it didn't do any good. My mother wasn't ready to make a truce yet. "You have better brothers than I have? Is that it? Finer men, more important, more prosperous, more respected, is that it?!" "Quiet now. Leave me alone," said my father, pulling his cap over his eyes and running out of the house. My father lost the battle. My mother remained the victor. She is always the victor. She wins every battle.

Uncle Hertz is not much better. He is the classic *shtetl nogid*, and shares the symbols of the Jewish rich, "the massive gold chain that rode around his paunch."

At the Purim feast itself, the family of poor relatives sits at Uncle Hertz's table terrified and silent, until one of the children is asked to sing a Purim song. The cracking voice brings forth spontaneous laughter from the other children, with the following results:

The first burst of laughter came from me, and it was I who caught the first slap from my mother. But the slap did not cool me off. It brought a burst of laughter from the other children, and from me as well. ... Another slap and fresh laughter and another slap and this went on until I was led out of the dining room into the kitchen and from the kitchen outdoors, and then I was brought home, beaten black and blue and drowning in tears. That night I cursed my own

bones and I cursed Purim and the Purim feast . . . and more
than anyone else I cursed Uncle Hertz, may he forgive me,
for he has long since passed on to his reward. On his grave
stands a tombstone, the most imposing tombstone in the
whole cemetery, and on it in gold letters are engraved the
virtues in which he excelled during his life: "Here lies . . .
kind-hearted, lovable, generous, charitable, good-tempered.
. . ." And so on and so on. . . . "May he rest in peace."

Thus our narrator reflects on a childhood singularly lacking
in maternal love and understanding, a childhood recalled
with pain and suffering. The tyranny of the family apparently
dominates his thoughts. Yet he seems to be able to cope rea-
sonably well with the trauma. Perhaps Sholom Aleichem
could not conceive of the kind of psychological marking
which became a characteristic of Jewish writers in the United
States half a century later. Indeed, there is very little in the
way of psychic probing in all of Yiddish fiction. Even the
brutal mother in "The Purim Feast" is, while an aberration
from the ideal matriarch, not presented as pathologically un-
balanced or unstable. The storyteller in "The Purim Feast"
stands before the tombstone of his uncle, reflecting on his
parents and his childhood, and we encounter none of the
overt neurotic activities or descriptions of, for example, an
Alex Portnoy, in Philip Roth's *Portnoy's Complaint,*[1] who
similarly feels compelled to talk about his childhood, an
overbearing Jewish mother and the associated traumatic
events of his youth. But Portnoy must confess to a psychia-
trist. The narrative comes from the perspective of the ana-
lyst's couch. In *shtetl* terms, this would be quite foreign. The
shtetl world, while having little interest in child psychology,
had even less interest in the mental (or sexual) problems of
adults.

The domineering mother figure was simply viewed as a
distortion of Jewish traditional law, which was spelled out in
the *Book of Proverbs*, Chapter 31: 10–31, in the concept of

the *Eshes Hayil* (Hebrew), "A Woman of Worth." What is described in *Proverbs* is the perfect housekeeper, the ideal complement to the husband, the perfect mother and wife. Her role is clearly defined in terms of support for her husband: "She does him good all the days of her life." In Sholom Aleichem's story "Gymnasia," the complaining narrator this time is the husband himself, who at the outset informs the reader of his problem: "Listen to me, your worst enemy can't do to you what you can do to yourself, especially if a woman —I mean a wife—interferes. . . . To look at her you might say she is a wife like all wives. . . . Really handsome, you might say, and not a fool, either. She is smart—very smart, you might say—in fact, a woman with a masculine brain." The mother has decided that their teenaged son will go to the *Gymnasia,* to the Gentile high school where he will be instructed in secular, non-Jewish subjects. She is prepared to move heaven and earth to have this happen and neither her husband nor her son has any voice in the decision. In fact, she invokes divine intervention in the creation of a situation which she realizes is not normal: " 'If God saw fit to put more brains into my little toe than into your whole head, I'm not to blame for that either.' 'How did we come around to that?' I asked. 'Very simply,' says she. 'Whenever there is a decision to be made around here, I am the one who has to rack her brains!' " When the husband suggests that perhaps a traditional Torah training might be just as good, she rages at him until he relents. After endless tribulations, hopes and disappointments, they finally gain admission to the *Gymnasia* for their son, in spite of quotas, disruptions, and even the loss of all their money. At the moment of the mother's triumph, the young son comes home from school to inform his parents that he has joined his classmates in a strike. For the first time the father asserts himself, urging the son to return to school, to think of all the sacrifice that the parents have made. But the mother explodes into the room and "lays down the law to me." Her message is that the son may do what he wishes; if he wants to strike, let him strike. This time the father's pleas are answered with a verbal assault on all sides: "She went after me . . . there was no end. . . . But she pays no attention to me. . . . Tell me, I beg you. Who ever invented wives?"

I. L. Peretz (1852–1915)

Peretz is inevitably linked to Mendele Mocher Sforim and to Sholom Aleichem to form the great troika of "classical" Yiddish literature. Chronologically and temperamentally, he belongs with them. He represents a different geographic and social audience, however. Peretz wrote primarily for Polish Jewry, and the historical events which produced this community of Jews were different from those which affected the Russian Jew. Poland had undergone a series of partitions during the eighteenth century, and many of her millions of Jews found themselves under Austrian rule. After the Congress of Vienna in 1815, the Jewish population had relatively settled down, and with the creation of the Austro-Hungarian monarchy and the reestablishment of the Polish state, Jews could finally be certain which government ruled them. No government in Poland in modern times was as repressive as that of the Czars, so Polish Jews had a considerably larger measure of emancipation and freedom than their Russian counterparts. Although poverty was endemic, there emerged in the nineteenth century a sizeable Jewish bourgeoisie, particularly in the major urban centers of Warsaw, Lublin, and Lodz. There were opportunities for education, and, although still an oppressed minority, Poland's Jews did not exist in a Pale. Even Hassidism in Poland took on a vigorously intellectual complexion, not unlike its northern Russian or Lithuanian branches.

This Yiddish literary flowering did not have quite the same

atmosphere of urgency which drove the Russian Jews to communicate with the masses in the Pale. Sholom Aleichem and Mendele were established Yiddish literary figures when Sholom Aleichem approached Isaac Leib Peretz and suggested that he might switch from Hebrew to Yiddish as his medium. When Peretz contributed to an edition of a Yiddish journal Sholom Aleichem was editing, he could do so under his own name; there was no longer a need to hide behind a pseudonym. Furthermore, Peretz's audience was not the *proste Yidn* of the Russian Pale, but the more sophisticated, often urban Jews of Poland. His stories are consistently more imaginative, his style more remote from the simple formulas of Sholom Aleichem. Peretz combined the traditional ideas of the Polish *shtetl* with his interest in mysticism and Hassidic fantasy to produce a fiction unique and distinctive.

Yet we encounter in Polish Jewry the same types, the same problems and formulas regarding family structure and tradition; while not with the same singular preoccupation as Mendele or Sholom Aleichem, Peretz nonetheless is very much concerned with the Jewish family. Like his two counterparts, he is also very much the Jewish writer-moralist. His most often anthologized story, "Devotion without End," is set not in a *shtetl,* but in a remote, romantic Palestine of centuries ago. But from the outset, from the opening paragraph, Peretz wants the reader to keep in mind the current scene: "There once dwelt in Safed a Jew of great wealth and good fortune, who traded in jewels, diamonds, and other precious stones. He was truly a man of great wealth, not like the upstarts of today." He takes this opportunity, while describing a Jew who lived hundreds of years ago, to slam the *nouveau riche* upstarts. Then Peretz goes on to describe that rarity in Yiddish literature, the good *nogid.*[2] This Jew is exemplary, giving freely of his wealth, studying and marrying his children into rabbinical families. His daughter Sarah, the youngest child, is betrothed to the brightest student in the Babylonian yeshiva, a young man named Chiya, who is also very modest. This kept son-in-law inherits the riches of the Jew of Safed when he dies, and Reb Chiya becomes one of the greatest merchants of his time, as well as a scholar and humanitarian known throughout the world. Peretz's intention in describing Reb Chiya and his wife Sarah is to provide a perfect model for the Jewish family. Sarah exemplifies the ideal *Eshes Hayil,* the ultimate *shtetl* wife:

> During the lengthy months and years that Reb Chiya was absent from home, his good wife Sarah would maintain the kind of household that did honor to a man of his standing. Reb Chiya had complete faith in her. He knew that the hungry would leave her door sated and the thirsty refreshed. And he knew that Sarah would raise their only daughter in the ways of piety and goodness.

Their daughter Miriam is a striking contrast to Tevye's rebellious children:

> Once Reb Chiya stopped his daughter Miriam, looked upon her with love and pity, and asked, "My daughter, do you ever visit your mother's grave?"
> "Yes," she answered.
> "And what do you pray for at your mother's grave?"
> Lifting her faithful eyes, she replied, "I pray for your health, my father. At times you seem so sad, and I, alas, know not how to gladden you. She, my mother, knew how. . . . I shall always heed you. . . ."

At the same time, Peretz is quick to show what he considers "abnormal" parental behavior, and once again we find it primarily attached to the widow. The young rabbinical student Chananiah, destined to become Miriam's husband, is at first a brilliant yeshiva student who is almost ruined, literally, by his mother's kisses: "The mother's heart was wholly given over to her son. . . . She wished to keep her darling at home. . . . The mother—for what can one expect from a fool-ish woman?—swelled with pride. . . . The head of the yeshiva sent word . . . that she should punish the boy, but instead the mother gave Chananiah a kiss and bought him a costly present." Chananiah indulges in the most negative kind of talmudic disputation, always destructive, besting other students in a harsh, dialectical debate which always ends in the humiliation of his opponent. The mother accepts this dissolute activity, called *pilpul* (Hebrew), "pepper," as a show of her son's brilliance, but Peretz condemns the abuse of Torah, and brings the mother to a harsh realization of her foolishness when the head of the yeshiva curses her son and makes him forget everything he had ever learned. Peretz, like his Russian fellow writer Sholom Aleichem, understood *shtetl* values thoroughly. A widowed woman, particularly one with money, was not a proper parent for a male child.

Second Generation Yiddish Writers

Yiddish literature was a literature in a hurry. It did not have the time or leisure to develop themes, modes or forms encountered in literary traditions that could unfold over a period of many generations. For Yiddish literature, almost incredibly, the second generation will prove to be the last one. Mendele died in 1917, Sholom Aleichem in 1916, and Peretz in 1915. By the time of their passing, the next generation (among them Sholem Asch, 1880–1957; Zalman Schneour, 1887–1959; I. J. Singer, 1893–1944) was already represented by mature writers. Two of the more prominent ones who are still alive today, I. B. Singer (1902–   ) and Chaim Grade (1910–   ), would still be reckoned as contemporaries of the three great classicists. Yet when they die, there is no sign at present that there will be Yiddish writers to carry on the tradition after them. While there are perhaps a handful of men and women still writing in Yiddish who are under the age of sixty, it would take a most convincing argument to demonstrate that Yiddish literature will still be alive in fifty years.

This makes its history all the more remarkable, because in two brief generations it produced a vibrant, fully developed literary heritage. It successfully left the source of its inspiration, the *shtetl,* and transplanted itself into a new world (both I. B. Singer and Grade are residents of New York City, Singer since 1935 and Grade since 1936). While never fully abandoning the values of the Old World, these second generation writers, nonetheless, brought a sophistication and a flexibility to their traditional attitudes which had to affect the stereotypes of *shtetl* preoccupations. The preoccupation with family life never changed, never left the center of Yiddish literary attention. But the more the writers of the second generation were exposed to the literary traditions of the West, the more these *shtetl* types took on characteristics encountered only rarely in the first generation writers. Mendele, Sholom Aleichem, and Peretz, for example, almost uniformly avoided erotic themes or any mention of sexuality. Also, although the classicists did confront issues of poverty, brutality, and change in the *shtetl,* there was still a certain delicacy which took into consideration the sensibilities of the Jewish masses. With the coming of the next generation of writers, there was less inhibition and more willingness to shock.

Sholem Asch is perhaps the most controversial figure who ever wrote in the Yiddish language. Born in Poland, he emigrated to America in 1914. By the time of his death in 1957, he had become the most translated writer in Yiddish literary history, and his works were well known in the United States. He also had been condemned as an apostate, particularly denounced in Hassidic circles, and was rumored to have been refused burial in a Jewish cemetery. The cause of Asch's problems was a series of novels which focused on the Jewish-Christian symbiosis, and particularly *The Apostle, Mary* and

The Nazarene, a life of Christ. Even in his more traditional Yiddish works Asch demonstrated a willingness to confront issues which the earlier writers either would avoid or which seemed too far from *shtetl* realities as they saw them. In *Mottke the Thief* Asch depicts an urban Jewish underworld fully the equal of any picaresque representation in other Western literatures. Even in his major novel, *Dos Shtetl,* the picture of Jewish life in a typical East European town is richer and more fully developed than in the shorter narratives of his predecessors. Asch was the first, perhaps the only major Yiddish writer who consistently preferred the longer narrative form and who mastered the novel-length work. As a result, his characters and situations are more fully fleshed out.

Above all, his works are marked by an aggressiveness which derives its power from his glorification of the lowest classes. Asch loved the proletariat, admired the strength of the Jews who worked, whenever possible, with their hands. He represents the first generation of Jews who were thoroughly gripped by the potential of Zionism as a movement which might totally regenerate the Jew and recreate those Jewish values which were associated with energy and strength before the Diaspora. For Asch, the hope of the future was the common man, and it was toward this segment of society that he directed his energies. But Asch would always be a Jew writing in Yiddish for other Jews, and as such he continued to focus on the drama he was certain would get the greatest attention: on the family.

Two of his stories graphically show the impact of ideas which now emerge in the fledgling but developing literature. "Sanctification of the Name" and "Kola Street" are stories of the new type of Jewish heroes. "Sanctification" is a tale of Jewish martyrdom. Four Polish Jews, the most prominent members of a *shtetl* community, are celebrating the marriage of one of their children, and while driving home on the snow-

covered road, encounter the carriage of the *Pan,* the noble-
man who rules their lives. In joyous drunkenness, they refuse
to give way on the highway, yell insults in Yiddish, and the
next morning all four are arrested—along with the driver of
their cart, a young Jewish drayman looked upon with suspicion by the community because of his contempt for his religion and his indifference to his fellows' reproaches. The
Jews are doomed to death unless they admit to having murdered a peasant, and then convert to Christianity. Those
that refuse will be beheaded. While the Jews of the *shtetl*
gather in the synagogue to pray and to sing psalms, they hear
the screams of the tortured men.

Asch deals with this situation with a mixture of traditional
Jewish determination in the face of such events and a grotesque horror at the willingness of the Jews to sacrifice their
loved ones. There is a special kind of ambiguity throughout
this bizarre tale. "In the lamentations of the wives and
mothers of the tormented ones there is never a suggestion of
a desire for weakness; when their eyes have wearied of
shedding tears they look forth into space with pride. And
when the women about them dare to look at them, their eyes
too betray pride, and even a reverent envy of the wives and
mothers of the men who are sanctifying the Name of God."

The community worries, however, about the young Jewish
driver, who on several occasions threatened to convert when
his elders insisted that he attend synagogue services. He
rides on Sabbath, and he is ignorant of the laws of Judaism.
His mother sits alone in the synagogue now, in a corner of
the women's gallery, receiving the glances from the other
women, and an occasional "To have brought forth such a
son! To have given such a son to the Jewish fold!" She, too,
like her son, is ignorant of Torah, and she has to accept responsibility for her son's expected apostasy. The others will
have nothing to do with her. "The others have withdrawn
from her. She says no Psalms, for she cannot read, she does

not know the text." The other women burn candles for the four expected martyrs, but refuse to allow the drayman's mother to burn her candle with theirs.

Then comes the news: the executions have taken place, and the heads are thrown against the synagogue door:

> One, two, three, four—five. Five knocks. And at the sound of the fifth the mother of the drayman springs from her place by the unlighted candle and tears open the door. Five heads lie on the ground before the synagogue door. She sought out the head of her son and lifted it in both hands. Holding it high before her, she entered the synagogue. It was as if she wanted the whole world to see. A fierce pride shone from her eyes. She had lifted the kerchief from her face, so that she might look back at everyone of the assembled. And the assembled moved away from her reverently, envy and wonder on their faces, made a space for her, when she began to dance. "The mother dances with her son! The mother dances with her son!"

Asch's treatment of the martyrdom of the renegade Jew and his mother's response borders on the gothic. The image of the Jewish mother filled with a sense of *naches,* of pleasure, while she dances with the head of her son as others look on with envy is one which would have been inconceivable in the Yiddish literary tradition of only a few years earlier. With one stroke, Asch has moved the *shtetl*-bound folk literature right into the mainstream of modern grotesque. At the same time, he focuses on the traditional Jewish themes of *yichus* within the social and familial structure of the community. It is still very much a story of parents and children, of husbands and wives. But it is also much more.

The only puzzling note concerns the attitude of the Jewish community toward the murder of their fellow Jews. For in the passive lamentations and prayers we encounter an attitude which Sholem Asch most certainly did not share. He was a militant, a believer in a new aggressiveness, a forceful believer in Jewish self-defense, not the mere traditional passivity of the *shtetl* which the Diaspora had taught for centuries. Sholem Asch wanted action, he wanted to create a New Jew, a Jew for the modern world, one who would not merely sit by and watch his family be slaughtered. With this specific purpose in mind, he wrote *Kola Street,* a tale filled with the excitement and energy of a new Jewish vitality. Once again, the energy is found in the common proletarians, the hard-working, dirt-under-the-nails Jews who understand little of Torah but know what it means to be a Jew. At the same time, he attacks those who in his mind represent the traditional image of Jewish nonaggressiveness: the Hassidim. The heroes live on Kola Street in an unnamed Jewish *shtetl* in Poland. "This street was not in the Diaspora, as it were; there no Jew was ever beaten." For the Jews of Kola Street represent Asch's celebration of Jewish vitality. There are fishermen, cattlemen, and horse dealers, strong, powerful, and proud. But they are also pious, if not terribly learned, and for their Torah they turn to the street of the scholars, where the Hassidim live:

> The street of the scholars, the street where lived the rabbi and the teachers, and where the bathhouse and the poultry slaughtering yard are situated, felt very much ashamed of Kola Street: "These illiterates, butchers, fishmongers!" The scholars lived entirely on the festival money contributed by Kola Street and whenever they were in trouble—whenever a shepherd set his dog on a Jew or a drunken peasant started a row in their street—Jews young and old would run to Kola Street, crying for help. Nevertheless, the scholars condemned Kola Street. "Not at all like Jews. . . . Savages with no manners at all. . . ."

It is just the fact that they are not like other Jews which makes them so admirable, for Asch contrasts them with the "Jews in black caftans" who run and hide during pogroms, and who, moreover, are conniving, double-dealing businessmen—*luftmenshen*—who steal from Jew and Gentile alike. The patriarch of Kola Street is Reb Israel, a giant with the wisdom of Solomon, but also a pious Jew who loves Rashi's commentaries. He marries his daughters to the best yeshiva students and then keeps them to the best of his ability, so that they may spend their lives in study: "His sons-in-law with their great volumes of the Talmud inspired him with such awe that he walked on tiptoe before them. He reserved for them the best and most precious of his possessions, and when he heard the voice of the Torah resounding in his house the old man wept for joy."

But as a father, Reb Israel had not imparted any measure of Judaism to his sons. They were robust like himself, but totally ignorant of the Law, and the strongest and most brazen of all was Notte, the child of his old age. Asch makes the father-son relationship the core of the dilemma in *Kola Street*; we are made to admire Reb Israel and his sons and Asch obviously has no sympathy for any of the scholars (including the sons-in-law), yet Notte's ignorance of Judaism and his clearly Gentile ways bring about the crisis in the story. First of all, he surrounds himself with animals. He is an accomplished rider, is always accompanied by his dog, and as a hobby he raises pigeons which rival those of the Gentile baker. Most flagrant of all, there is Josephine, the Gentile housekeeper whom Reb Israel had brought into the house as a youngster. Now a strapping woman, she is obviously more than just a servant girl to Notte. He beats her, which she does not seem to mind. "When she saw him on his horse, she walked out in front of the house and stood with arms akimbo, her eyes smiling through the red and blue welts he had left on her face. 'There's no rider like him!' . . . and quickly followed Notte upstairs." Asch admits to the *shtetl* world a note of sexuality which hitherto was unknown. The *shtetl* inhabitants for whom Sholom Aleichem wrote were prepared to confront the Jewish-Gentile boy-meets-girl tragedy because it was a fact which they lived with. In matters of sex or erotic fantasy, however, the average *shtetl* dweller was something of a puritan. The combination of Asch's more urbane audience and his own sophistication produced an environment different from that of the earlier writers.

It was inevitable that Jewish writers would turn more directly to sexual themes, and I. J. Singer's story, "Sand," while holding firmly to the *shtetl* preoccupation with family, honor, and tradition, integrates erotic themes in a way peculiarly suited to the forms and content of Yiddish literature. This Jewish Romeo and Juliet story of the rivalry of two towns—the proletarian, good-natured but ignorant Jews of Podgurna and the arrogant, learned, and small-minded Jews of Grobitze—explores the sensual feelings of two young people. The granddaughter of the Podgurna village teacher, Mashka is a young woman awakening to her own sexuality:

> Mashka goes out into the sand, pulls her dress up over her knees, and dances. There is no one to see. She opens her blouse and shows first the whiteness of her throat, and then one little breast, and as her dancing grows wilder and her blouse opens more, the other little breast. She puts her hands up to her young breasts, very tenderly, as if she were holding two young kittens to her heart. Suddenly she sees her shadow on the sand, imitating every gesture of hers, and she is ashamed.

Her admirer is Aaron, a ritual slaughterer from Grobitze, who comes to Podgurna to kill cattle for the army. Singer prepares the reader for the pivotal scene in which the young couple consummate their love in a stunning *tour de force* of specifically Jewish erotica. He combines the act of the *shoychet,* the priestly killing of animals as described in the Pentateuch, with the imagery of sexual arousal:

> 'Faster there, Aaron! That's enough testing the knife. The soldiers don't mind how you kill!' He moves faster from

one outstretched throat to another: a light swift motion of
the knife, back and forth, then he tries to jump clear of
the hot breath and the spouting blood. The screaming and
gurgling grow louder ... Not far from the animals that still
spout blood, barefoot village girls kneel with shallow tin
bowls, catching whatever blood they can. They carry the
blood home and cook it. The young men take no money,
but now and then one of them lays bloody hands on a girl
and drags her away to a corner of the slaughterhouse. . . .
Then something boils up in Aaron; he feels the veins in his
eyes growing hot, and there is a tingling at the roots of his
hair. He sets his teeth and rolls his sleeves higher; he feels
his anger rising at the sight of the outstretched throats and
glaring eyes of the oxen, and his knife slides faster, bites
deeper. When the day's work is over he comes to visit Reb
Jonah.

This is a description which has its full significance only in
the frame of reference of Jewish literature; Singer joins the
holy and the profane and consecrates the act of sex.

The story has a happy ending, thanks to Podgurna's respected patriarch, the sturdy Pesach Plotnik, another of Yiddish literature's physical and fundamentally wise men.
Singer, like Asch, glorifies those earthy, strong characteristics in Jewish men to counteract the stereotyped image of
the cowering *Hassid* hiding under a table during a pogrom.
When Mashka gives birth to an illegitimate child, Podgurna
is shamed and Grobitze celebrates in a fit of *Schadenfreude,*
the peculiar glee we experience at other people's troubles.
The women of Podgurna are particularly cruel to Mashka,
since her fall, they feel, is a reflection on all of them. They
are just about to curse Mashka and her bastard child when
Plotnik enters the synagogue, throws out all the women and
children, and sends word throughout the village: Mashka is
to be treated with respect. After a bloody nose, Aaron agrees
to the wedding, and the ceremony takes place at the same
time that the child is circumcised.

As in Asch's "Kola Street," Singer here shows a proper kind of balance between following the letter of religious law and street wisdom. There are no rabbinical decisions or interpretations on bastard children, laws of legitimacy, or the like. With his mighty right fist Pesach Plotnik has decided, and everything works out. Again, the scholars give way to the physically strong Jews who also possess more than a small measure of wisdom. Again, it is the Jew of the soil who emerges heroically.

But the world of the *proste,* the common Jew, was not always glorified. The Yiddish writer was also capable of describing the most sordid lower depths, Jewish families in a harshly naturalistic setting in which the ties of parenthood are barely recognizable. Such is the case in Zalman Schneour's (1887–1959) "The Girl." The tradition of the simple creatures of God, the *lamed vavs* or thirty-six just men, was, as already mentioned, part of *shtetl* lore. The simpleton always received a special measure of respect, even if only in the afterlife, as in the case of Peretz's famous "Bontsha the Silent," the story of a sainted fool who receives his rewards in paradise. I. B. Singer's Gimpel is scorned and ridiculed by the community, but the reader is fully aware that for the fool God reserves a unique role. However, in Schneour's story Brayne is almost pathologically retarded. Bontsha's silence seemed imposed on him as part of his role; Brayne grunts like an animal; indeed, Schneour's description is that of a dumb brute: "No one could possibly call Brayne a girl—just the Girl. Her parents called her the Girl, her neighbors called her the Girl. Even strangers, seeing her for the first time, immediately thought of her as the Girl. A hulking creature, she had fiery red cheeks under small greasy green eyes, and pendulous blue lips. Her fat hands were always red ... Tall, thick, unyielding, clumsy as a chunk of wood. ..." Her parents come from the pits of the *shtetl* society, a world so grim that it could perhaps produce nothing else but a creature such as Brayne. Her mother Asne is a small, bitter, cursing woman who freezes all day in the market place, selling a few pennies' worth of poppy seeds. The father Zavel is an old drunkard who rarely gets off the sofa, and throws his shoes at his hulking child while throwing curses at the same time. Schneour presents us with the picture of these two tiny, mean-spirited people dancing around their idiot child, "smashing her and sticking her while she silently blinks her eyes, sweat and snuffle, an exhausted horse."

But Schneour's main purpose is to explore the awakening sexual feelings of this creature. It is a theme which the turn-of-the-century European Naturalists pursued, particularly in the environment which Schneour creates, one dominated by economic deprivation, alcoholism, the very lowest classes of society, even muted imbecility. Brayne, during an occasional moment of rest, would sit at the window and watch the young couples walk by: "Inside of her something tugged and ached, and she laughed. Odd laughter—a queer noise from her chest and a stifled giggle—laughter like a hen's cries. . . . How could such a small, smothered sound come from a great healthy cow like Brayne?"

Her "suitor" is a local Jewish degenerate, Benny Lip, so named because of a birth defect. The courtship is consistent with the almost grotesque nature of their grim lives. The young Jewish thief comes by to purchase a few pennies' worth of poppy seeds, pinches Brayne and drives her into howls of excitement before he leaves. Once a year Zavel goes to the synagogue to say a prayer for his dead parents, and on returning one evening he finds Benny Lip leaving Brayne. The next day, when mother and father begin their customary beating, "the most astonishing thing happened. Instead of humbly receiving the blows, Brayne ran about the room, her red, dough-covered fists clenched, her teeth bared, and roared like an animal, 'Oo-oo-oo!' Zavel paled. For the first time he recognized in Brayne a creature stronger than himself." Relations between parents and child now change. Zavel ceases throwing shoes at his daughter, the beatings stop, and instead the parents let out their frustrations in a stream of abusive curses, but they keep their distance from the now menacing Brayne. Zavel drinks more, Asne continues to freeze in the market, Benny Lip no longer comes around, and inevitably, Brayne reveals the signs of her pregnancy. The story ends with parents and child in utter despair.

The reader is never permitted access to Brayne's thoughts. We study her from the outside, and Schneour permits us to see no more than the girl's moronic sexual urges as they develop within the wretched family situation in the grimmest of shtetls. The very same ingredients are present in I. B. Singer's "Gimpel the Fool," except that the cruelty emanates not from the family but from the surrogate family, in this case the shtetl itself. Singer takes the extraordinary step of letting the fool tell his own story. Gimpel is an orphan, and as such a ward of the community. But the shtetl of Frampol is made up of malicious types who prefer to have their pleasure at Gimpel's expense. "I am not a slugger by nature," admits Gimpel, who would rather smile and accept the taunts of his townsmen.[3] They go so far as to force a marriage on him with Elka, the town whore, whom Gimpel describes: "Her mouth would open as if it were on a hinge, and she had a fierce tongue. I entered the house. She was dressed in a worn hand-me-down gown of plush. She had her hair put up in braids and pinned across her head. It took my breath away, almost, the reek of it." The shtetl community's malevolence contrasts with the almost childlike innocence of Gimpel. Only the old rabbi is generous to him, and when Elka bears him a son seventeen weeks after the marriage, Gimpel seeks advice from him, and the rabbi insists on a divorce. But Gimpel is too good-natured to wish to leave Elka; she continues to have children while the town mocks poor Gimpel. "All Frampol refreshed its spirits because of my trouble and grief." Elka's infidelities go on; there are six children after twenty years of marriage, and on her death-bed, consumed by cancer, Elka begs Gimpel for forgiveness: none of the children are his.

Gimpel now wrestles with the spirit of evil which comes to him at night, to tempt him to urinate into the bread dough which he is preparing for the morning. He commits this sin in a fit of anger, but a vision of Elka with her face burnt black by the fires of hell causes him to bury the defiled loaves in the frozen earth. The next morning, Gimpel divides his savings among his children, packs his prayer shawl and says goodbye to Frampol. He is beginning his quest, an itinerant mendicant-*shnorrer* searching for the nature of truth and reality. He dreams for many years of Elka and waits for the time he may join her: "The grave waits and the worms are hungry; the shrouds are prepared—I carry them in my beggar's sack. Another *shnorrer* is waiting to inherit my bed of straw. When the time comes, I will go joyfully. Whatever may be there, it will be real, without complication, without ridicule, without deception. God be praised: there even Gimpel cannot be deceived."

Singer's genius transcends the limitations of the *shtetl* experience while at the same time drawing from this experience. Without parents, Gimpel can expect that the *shtetl* might assume responsibility for at least his early years. This is the tradition of the Jewish community, an early manifestation of shared social welfare, with something—even very little, but at least something—for all. In Gimpel's case, we see the mean-spirited community, almost sadistic in its pleasure in tormenting the innocent. This is family in the largest sense, for the *shtetl* understood the nature of the duty to the orphan; it was an obligation, a commandment, a *mitzvah*. In this setting, Singer is actually writing about mankind's inherent savagery, as well as its ignorance. For Gimpel is genuinely the sainted fool, blessed not only with a solid faith in God—shaken for a moment, to be sure—but with a fundamental belief in humanity. The community takes him for a fool because he is a "believer"; he accepts even the most outrageous stories because, after all, if one believes that the Messiah will come, why not accept the stories of the villagers? His ultimate faith is in his wife, and as the *shlemihl*-husband who takes unspeakable abuse during his life Gimpel is a martyr to the institution of marriage. But in Singer's world, Elka gets her just reward, the fires of hell. She emerges as a better wife after death; her visitations to Gimpel while he waits for his end are marked by a consideration which she did not demonstrate in life. Gimpel also has to experience humanity on a scale larger than Frampol, so Singer puts him on the road as a wanderer, to discover perhaps that the world outside is not as cruel as Frampol. He rediscovers the innocence of children, becomes an itinerant storyteller, reaffirms his will to believe in mankind. As he awaits the end, there is still the bewildered innocent, certain of one thing, however, that God will call him, and that Gimpel will no longer be deceived.

Singer has broken out of the *shtetl* stereotype while building on the foundations of *shtetl* tradition. Gimpel is much more than the *lamed vav* or the weak husband, or the abused orphan. Singer has created here an allegory which is free from the limitations imposed by the traditions of a private Jewish world. In the Bellow translation, Singer became a voice for all mankind.

From Old World to New World: I. B. Singer's "The Little Shoemakers"

There were aspects of Singer's fictional world which prevented him from attaining, in the Yiddish world, the popularity which he came to enjoy in the American, English-speaking one. He did violate some of the taboos of the *shtetl* world. In "Gimpel the Fool," when Gimpel attempts to consummate his marriage with Elka, she tells him she is "having my monthlies." Such outspoken mention of menstruation was a guarantee to alienate the average Jewish audience, no matter how mature it had become during the second generation of Yiddish literature. Also, if we recall the deaths of Golde in the Tevye stories, and Reb Chiya's wife Sarah in "Devotion without End" we discover the accepted, modest manner of death, particularly for women, in *shtetl* terms. Singer, remember, arrived in America in 1935, and was writing for an American-Jewish population that was already growing older. His description of Elka's end begins with a small growth on her breast which ultimately develops into cancer; death by cancer was certainly not a subject acceptable to his readership. Finally, Singer's approach to the occult and mystical aspects of Judaism was vastly different from that of Peretz, who created material visions of the afterlife with Moses-like judges, pearly gates, and the like. Singer's world is one of imps, devils, faces burned by the flames of *Gehenna,* and similar strange apparitions. In short, he created a fictive world which responded neither to the needs of the old-world Jew nor the new-world Jew.

Occasionally, Singer would clearly create a world for no other purpose than to appeal to his audience after 1935, the Jewish reader now increasingly located on the Lower East Side of New York, a group of people whom we shall deal with in greater detail in the next chapter. "The Little Shoemakers" is a story of the transition of Jews from Europe to America; it is hopelessly sentimental, and at the same time an accurate measurement of the hopes and dreams of the Jew who has created a new *shtetl* for himself on the lower end of Manhattan Island. Even more significant, it clearly shows the disintegration of the European *shtetl* at the very last moment of its existence, as Hitler's hordes were sweeping over Poland.

While a short story, Singer's tale has a distinctly epochal flavor. It is the history of many generations of the Shuster family, shoemakers who came to Frampol at the time of the Chmielnitski massacres of 1648. For two hundred and fifty years, the Shusters of Frampol made good shoes, lived the lives of pious men and women, and bore generations of sturdy children, mostly boys. Toward the end of the nineteenth century, the patriarch of the family is Abba Shuster, named for the founder, a man of tradition, good, kind, and possessing all the nobility of his world. As he grows old, he looks around, sees his seven fine sons, and is satisfied with his life: "No, this was good enough for Abba Shuster. There was nothing to change. Let everything stand as it had stood for ages, until he lived out his allotted time and was buried in the cemetery among his ancestors, who had shod the sacred community and whose good name was preserved not only in Frampol but in the surrounding district."

One can only imagine the shock and disbelief when his eldest son Gimpel announces that he is going to America. Abba's reply perfectly reflects the attitude of his generation. "What happened? Did you rob someone? Did you get into a fight?" For the Jews of Poland, not living under the yoke of Czarist oppression, life could be modestly pleasant, and the Shuster family had made, for them, an acceptable adjustment to centuries in a land which they no longer viewed as adopted. Poland was home, the ancestral country of their origin. Abba could not understand why anyone would want to leave. When Gimpel gives as a reason the fact that he has no future, the father replies: "Why not? You know a trade. God willing, you'll marry someday. You have everything to look forward to." What follows is a totally different perception of *shtetl* life, one seen from the perspective of those willing to

go, to pull up roots and leave. There is no hint of romanti-
cism, of the later nostalgia. Gimpel's outburst represents a
picture of *shtetl* life stripped of any positive feature:

> The boy spoke up, but Abba couldn't understand a word of
> it. He laid into synagogue and state with such venom, Abba
> could only imagine that the poor soul was possessed: the
> Hebrew teachers beat the children, the women empty their
> slop pails right outside the door, the shopkeepers loiter in
> the streets, there are no toilets anywhere and the public
> relieves itself as it pleases, behind the bathhouse or out in
> the open, encouraging epidemics and plagues. He made fun
> of Ezreal the healer and of Mecheles the marriage broker,
> nor did he spare the rabbinical court and the bath atten-
> dant, the washerwoman and the overseer of the poorhouse,
> the professions and the benevolent societies.

Here is an indictment which leaves no hope of improvement;
the only way out is to abandon, and Gimpel leaves home.
Abba sees a train for the first time when he takes his son to
the station in the next town. "He took the headlights of the
locomotive for the eyes of a hideous devil." As the boy
leaves, Abba cries after him: "Don't forsake your religion!"
Of course, Abba is convinced that his son will now fall away
from Judaism, so he is thoroughly relieved when a letter arrives after a few months, chronicling the illegal border crossing, a four-week ocean voyage, and the first sights of New
York. In the letter Singer symbolically joins the two worlds
for one final moment, the superstition and unchanging medievalism of the past—Gimpel writes that he had seen no
mermaids or mermen and had not heard them singing—with
the image of the free Jew—"The Gentiles speak English. No
one walks with his eyes on the ground, everybody holds his
head high." Gimpel is already showing the signs of belonging,
of identifying with the pride and energy of the immigrant in
America. Furthermore, he is quickly losing the image of "the
greenhorn," the newly arrived Jew who still carried with him

the sartorial and linguistic baggage of the *shtetl.* He now wears a short coat (unlike the Hassidim), and he informs his father in this letter, written, of course, in Yiddish, that he is working as a shoemaker and is *all right.* The last phrase appears alien to Abba's eyes; it is written with the familiar Yiddish letters, that is, the Hebrew alphabet, but it makes no sense to him: what does *all right* mean in Yiddish? Obviously, it was a new kind of Yiddish, a Yiddish unfamiliar to Abba. Gimpel had become an *allrightnik,* a Jew from the *shtetl* who was making out in America, and who was quickly adding little touches of English to his native Yiddish.

In the next letter Gimpel informs his family that he has met a woman from Rumania named Bessie, and they are engaged. She works *at dresses.* Again the foreign phrase with the familiar alphabet. The third letter contains a picture of the wedding which must have been like thousands of similar photographs in Europe and America, which were placed on bureaus or forgotten in the corners of drawers for generations, to be dug out during the past few years as a wave of nostalgia swept America. "Abba could not believe it. His son was wearing a gentleman's coat and a high hat. The bride was dressed like a countess in a white dress, with train and veil; she held a bouquet of flowers in her hand." Gimpel is a participant in the great wave of immigration which produced similar wedding photographs, a world of two-dollar rentals for tuxedos and wedding gowns, of a new *yichus* and status, in terms that were distinctly American now.

Within a matter of a few months all of Abba's children come to America, and the children beg their father to join them, but his world is still Frampol, and he wishes to end his life there. His wife, the faithful Pesha (the perfect *shtetl* wife once again!) dies, and forty years go by. Abba is now an ancient relic; *shtetl* life has not disintegrated; it simply has been forgotten. He spends his time sitting at his wife's grave, reading letters from the children now grown to manhood.

There are grandchildren, even great-grandchildren. The world apparently has passed Abba by, and he is quietly and contentedly waiting for his time.

But Abba did not reckon with Hitler's armies, and the modern world remembers the old man. Dive bombers suddenly (and most unlikely) attack Frampol, and Abba finds himself, with a few of his tools, on the road, a refugee. By the enormous effort of his sons, he is located, taken to Italy via Rumania, and sails on the last ship leaving for the United States. The crossing is a maze of images for the old, confused man, who is barely aware of his destination. As the ship docks at New York he is overwhelmed by boys, girls, men and women, talked to "in a strange language, which was both Yiddish and not Yiddish." In short, he had arrived.

Singer now will create a world of *naches* for the Jew in America, one still measured in terms of status, but a status distinctly of the American-Jewish experience. This is a story which the author writes with a specific audience in mind: that aging generation of Yiddish speakers and readers who want this time not problems, but solutions for their problems, as they see their children beginning to benefit from what is both the blessing and the curse of *shtetl* life in America: freedom. What occurs in Singer's story is as close to real life as these people wish to come; it emphasizes the pleasant and minimizes the unpleasant.

The description of the sons' lives in America is the perfect dream for the immigrant parent. All seven families live together, in seven homes surrounded by gardens, in what for this period of the 1930s and 1940s was the ultimate in *yichus*: Elizabeth, New Jersey. They are the owners of a successful shoe company, live happily together (no family squabbles, a later theme of American-Jewish fiction, in this story). There is to be a welcoming celebration in Gimpel's house, "in full compliance with the dietary laws; the meat was kosher, and a completely new set of dishes and utensils had been provided to prevent the least infraction of these laws." Singer goes out of his way to provide a picture of domestic and ritual perfection. The entire family is present, and, although the great numbers of young people speak a different language, the old man can bask in the warmth of his family. Ironically, Singer includes a "colored maid" in this mosaic, as a further reflection of the status of the Shuster family. This is, of course, the *shvartse,* who, like the Polish or Russian peasant, was a measure of whatever status the Jew might enjoy in relation to the Gentile world. The *Shabbes Goy,* the Sabbath Gentile who came to do the chores forbidden to the Jew, is transposed into the black maid, who becomes in Jewish-American *shtetl* lore an almost standard stereotype of prosperity.

Old Abba, however, does not thrive in this new, strange environment. His senses are disordered, he can barely walk, and in Gimpel's house he often would be found lost in some closet. Singer is going to the heart of the problem of aging for the *shtetl* Jew in America. In Frampol, Abba made shoes; in America, he is superfluous, an old man without a profession, and inevitably one of the daughters-in-law suggests a solution which undoubtedly Singer's readers had encountered all too frequently and which was becoming almost a way of life for the increasingly prosperous American Jew: "It wouldn't be such a bad idea to put him in a home." Singer can employ a theme which simply never existed in the *shtetl* Yiddish literature of, for example, Sholom Aleichem. There was no old age home in the normal sense in the Jewish community, although there might have been a *Moyshev Zkeynim,* literally, a home for the old, but this was generally for those few old people who did not have loved ones or *mishpoche* to care for them. The Jewish extended family was a three-generation structure: grandparents, parents, and children. As long as it was possible for all to live under one roof, it was done. It was a loss of esteem for all if any one of these parts

113

left. The aged and infirm were taken care of within the framework of the family. In America, this eventually changed with the movement away from the confines and self-imposed limitations of *shtetl*-ghetto life. Once the Jews—and Italians, Irish, and other ethnic groups—spilled out into suburbia, as often as not the orthodox old people were not able to adapt: it frequently meant walking miles to the nearest synagogue if they wanted to remain orthodox in spite of their children's often lax observance of Jewish ritual. This is the situation in which we find old Abba. Disoriented in his son's home in suburbia, out of step and out of pace with the life around him, generally "in the way," he is in every sense superfluous, even an embarrassment, no less so than Tevye was to his pompous son-in-law Padhatzur. But Singer will not tolerate such a grim solution in this contrived and delightful story. One day, shortly after the suggestion had been made that they put the old man away, he accidentally walked into a closet to discover his shoemaker's tools from Frampol, which he had taken on his hazardous journeys. He picked up an old shoe and began working:

> That day Abba did not lay in bed dozing. He worked busily till evening, and even ate his usual piece of chicken with greater appetite. He smiled at the grandchildren and they came in to see what he was doing. . . . The activity soon proved to be the old man's salvation. . . . He mended every last pair of shoes in the house. . . . He took on new life and looked fifteen years younger.

Continuing in the best and most direct traditions of Yiddish literature, Singer comes on with a direct message for the Jew growing old in America: keep your hands busy and your mind alert. There is no retirement village or old age home for Abba. He rediscovers the beauty of hand labor, of activity. His repaired shoes become the talk of the neighborhood, and a small hut is built in the backyard by his excited children.

There is still another, even more significant dimension to Abba's rebirth: "He even whittled a stylus and began to instruct them in the elements of Hebrew and piety." He rebuilds the old world connection with his grandchildren and great-grandchildren. The story ends as Abba looks at his middle-aged sons and the host of young ones running around enthusiastically in the gardens, and thinks: "No, praise God, they had not become idolators in Egypt. They had not forgotten their heritage, nor had they lost themselves among the unworthy."

Singer has written the perfect Jewish fairy tale for the Jew growing old in America. Assimilation has taken place only insofar as to provide a new kind of *yichus* (the elegant suburban home in New Jersey and the successful business enterprise in this case); in reality, no different from what the Jew had hoped for in Russia. The threat of total Americanization and loss of Jewish identity has been triumphantly beaten back; the little ones are learning Hebrew, and, indeed, it is the older generation which assumes the responsibility. Finally, old age in America can be beautiful as long as you keep busy and have understanding children. But in his efforts to create the Jewish paradise in America, Singer self-consciously underlines the problems for the former Kasrilevkites, the inhabitants of the *shtetls* of the old world who knew how to survive in a hostile environment, but who must face the challenge of prosperity in America with increasing anxieties.

6
Yiddishkeit on Two Continents

THE prosperity described so ideally by Singer in "The Little Shoemakers" was certainly not the experience of the vast majority of those millions of Jews who made their way from Russia after 1881, but it was a suitable dream nonetheless. Even more uncharacteristic, however, was the reestablished, traditional *shtetl* extended family, three generations of Jews living together, with all of the *mishpoche* within hailing distance. As the nineteenth century ended and the twentieth began, the Jewish family now found itself stretched and extended as it had not been since the Diaspora. Sons like Gimpel came over to America, but others stayed behind, and scarcely a Jewish family could be found that did not have relatives on both sides of the Atlantic.

Although this essay is primarily concerned with the development of the world of Yiddishkeit in America, in order to understand that experience for the American Jew we must still consider those who did not come over, those who represented the continuation of the Old World in the very places which were experiencing the upheavals of the modern age. For the fact remains that the majority of Jews stayed behind, spread throughout Europe, but concentrated in Russia, Poland, and Germany.

The Polish Jew, as has been mentioned earlier, lived in much better circumstances than his Russian brethren. Divided between Congress Poland and Austria-controlled Galicia, he never experienced, in modern times, the full weight of oppression as the Russian Jew did under Czarist regimes. The earliest waves of emigration from Eastern Europe came for the most part from Russia, not from Poland. From 1881 to 1905, the motives that the Russian Jews had for leaving were not necessarily shared by Galician Jews, although the economic plight of most Jews was just as grim as that of the Polish proletariat. Gradually, after the turn of the century, the trickle from Poland grew and reached the proportions of a wave with the outbreak of World War I and the subsequent disruptions of borders. These cataclysmic events also brought hundreds of thousands of other Polish Jews to America.

The outbreak of the First World War also caused disruptions for Germany's six hundred thousand Jews, but in a different manner. With the shattering of the Polish-German border in 1914, thousands of Polish refugee Jews in long black caftans and black beards, speaking a strange, outrageous German, poured into the towns and cities of eastern Germany. The German Jews were shocked to discover these aliens in their midst who described themselves as fellow Jews. They did everything they could to close the offending border, and Jewish agencies instituted a program called *Judensperre,* a Jewish blockade in effect, to keep the Hassidim out of Germany.

For the German Jew had indeed come a long way by 1914. The effects of the post-Mendelssohn period had produced the most assimilated and fully integrated Jewish community in western Europe. The Jew in Germany thought of himself as a German; he was fully a part of the Reich, generally a supporter of emperor and fatherland, conservative in taste, middle-class in values. He could be a passionate Wagnerite in spite of the open hostility of that most anti-Semitic of all composers. The language of the German Jew was German, exclusively. Yiddish had been, for more than a century, a dead language in Germany. When the First World War erupted, the German-Jewish volunteers fought in greater proportions than their non-Jewish countrymen. Although orthodoxy had not been wiped out, the Reform movement had captured the larger share of the German-Jewish population. It was, among other things, a means of appearing even more German, less Jewish. In Hamburg, one congregation decided to celebrate the Sabbath on Sunday, and soon others followed suit. Radical Reform Judaism ended the laws of *kashruth* (of keeping kosher), and created a Judaism which, with the exception of a very few regulations, could pass for Protestantism.

It is understandable that these fully assimilated Germans were stunned, in 1914, at the sight of their "brethren" who freely, in the best traditions of the East European *shtetl* world, asked for help from their fellow Jews. After a period of genuine hostility, this help finally appeared.

The German Jew did not participate in the migration to America along with the East European Jews. He was a German and belonged in Germany. His Zionism was only rhetorical. Martin Buber had said, after all: "When I talk of Zionism, I smell pine needles, not palm trees." For Buber, it was enough to talk of Zionism; the thought of actually moving to Palestine or to a Jewish homeland outside of Germany did not have much meaning for him, certainly not at the turn of the century, when he was a vital part of the German intellectual scene, a friend and confidant of many of the leading literary and philosophical personalities of the day.

The German Jew did not even feel himself threatened by the overt anti-Semitism of many of the political parties in Weimar Germany after the end of hostilities and the establishment of the German republic in 1919. One of these parties was the National Socialist Workers' Party, the Nazis. And ranged alongside the Hitler party was a whole group of other fascist-like organizations, all of which shared a common anti-

118

Jewish bias. For them, as for the Nazi Party, Germany's misfortune was its Jews. They were blamed for the loss of the war, for the establishment of the hated republic, and for the abominable Treaty of Versailles, which sealed Germany's humiliation. The Jews did organize some defensive organizations, but the general feeling was that eventually all of this would disappear, that it was the result of the frustration of losing the war. The German Jew considered that, in spite of this temporary set-back, he could count on his loyalty and his sense of Germanness to pull him through. In fact, Hitler, in spite of his rhetoric on "The Jewish Problem," always managed to receive 7 to 8 percent of the Jewish vote. There was always a small percentage of Jews who assumed that Hitler's rantings were directed against "them," the Eastern Jews, not against "us." They shared with Hitler a kind of anti-Semitism, they felt that their own *yichus* as Germans was affected by the presence of the Hassidic strangers in their midst, and wanted no part of non-German Jews. It was this segment, tiny as it was, that consistently voted for the Nazi party, not to mention the other reactionary parties which made up both the left and the right in Weimar Germany during the 1920s.

Even with the assumption of power of Nazism in Germany in January 1933, the German Jews were for the most part convinced that "it was just a fad; wait, it will pass," and they decided to hold on until the Germans came to their senses. There are ghastly stories of German Jews lining up at attention in concentration camps, in military formation, determined to show their Gestapo tormentors that they were better and more orderly Germans than those black-uniformed SS upstarts.

Some naturally saw the truth immediately and began migrating out of Germany even before Hitler's coming to power. But for the most part, German Jewish emigration continued at a slow pace in spite of the Nuremberg racial laws of 1934.

With the Nazi Olympics of 1936, many of those who felt that Nazism was only a temporary aberration felt vindicated: Hitler had told the world that Jews would be able to participate on the German team. None did, but the Jewish community in Germany saw that message as an effort at compromise.[1] But as soon as the Olympics were over, anti-Semitism came back with vigor, and the German Jews were persecuted, placed in the concentration camps, and deprived of their rights. Still there was a persistent feeling that better times would come. Not until the infamous Crystal Night in November 1938, when all of Germany's synagogues were destroyed, did it become clear that Hitler had something very special in mind for "his Jews," as he liked to refer to them. By then, those who could get out were trying to escape, via France, China, Russia, or anywhere.

Ultimately, several hundred thousand did manage to get out, while others tragically shared the same fate as their fellow Jews all over Europe. Yet Hitler was remarkably clever. He understood the sensibilities of the German Jews, the sense of separateness which was a built-in means for their own exploitation. People like Adolf Eichmann, who could speak perfect Yiddish and who felt he understood "Jewish" psychology, urged Hitler to exploit the sense of *yichus*. There were thousands of German Jews who to the very last moment were trying to convince the Nazis that they were different, racially and spiritually different from the Eastern Jews. During the years before the Final Solution, Hitler manipulated the German Jews, at times taking them into his confidence, playing on their sense of German nationalism. It was not until well into 1940 that the German Jew was forced to wear the Star of David on his clothing. Hitler turned the screw with discrimination, until it was psychologically advantageous for him to turn it all the way.

Even after the Holocaust, the German Jew remains something of an enigma, someone apart, with his own measurement of status. In the stiflingly prejudiced air of the American fraternity system immediately after the Second World War, with the smell of the ovens still in everyone's nostrils, one encountered, in American universities, the phenomenon of the German-Jewish fraternity that would not pledge Jews from Eastern Europe. In Israel today, there are Kibbutzim where the language of conversation and daily activity is still German, where colonies of immigrant Germans still keep very much to themselves, celebrating, we are told, the birthdays of emperors and Kaisers! [2]

The Tragedy of Yiddish in Soviet Russia

The grim history of the Jew in Germany in the twentieth century has really nothing to do with Yiddish literary traditions or even *shtetl* life. As has been said before, Yiddish was a dead language in Germany; no respectable German Jew would admit that he could understand a word of it.[3] The opposite was true in Russia, however. In spite of massive emigration, *Yiddishkeit* remained a vital force in Czarist as well as Soviet Russia. Even after the millions of Jews had left Czarist Russia, a major literary heritage was left behind which blossomed and flourished during the halcyon days of the Soviet regime, and which ultimately experienced a martyrdom not unlike that suffered by the masses under the Nazis.

When the revolution broke out in 1917, there was considerable Jewish participation, and during the period of civil war, the Jewish population suffered enormous hardships. The White armies once again found in the Jew a perfect scapegoat, and pogroms took place wherever Jews could be found.[4] But the atmosphere during the first years of the Bolshevik government was a happy one for Yiddish writers. Taking their inspiration from those writers who looked to Peretz in Warsaw for their inspiration, another group in Kiev (Sholom Aleichem's Yehupetz!) began transforming Yiddish literary ideas to the needs and ideals of the new life around them. The revolution was still alive and in the air, and this first generation of genuinely political and literary activists wanted to be part of it. "The promise of Socialism" presented previously inconceivable opportunities for Russia's Jews. As in the past, however, the obstacles which slowed down the potential progress of the Jews were the same ones which offended the *maskilim* of a previous generation: the *shtetl* had been hammered at, pillaged and burned, but it still was there, still a factor to be reckoned with, still inhabited by millions of Tevyes and *Hassidim* who had not pulled up, but who had stayed behind and were determined to resist change. The challenge excited the young Soviet Yiddishists, and they turned to it with energy and talent. Still writing in Yiddish, they wished to communicate to these Jews what the revolution could mean to them, and furthermore, that the traditional *shtetl* ways were destined to be swept away in the cause.[5]

The early euphoria soon disappeared under Stalinist repression, and the Yiddishists were caught up in the increasing anti-Semitism of the Russian leader. The important and imaginative Yiddish writers in the Soviet Union were, by the mid-1920s, under attack for revisionism, and the early support which the government had given to Yiddish expression disappeared. By the mid-1930s wholesale purges were underway which swallowed up many great Yiddish writers, who simply disappeared, never to be heard from again. When the Nazi threat came to the Soviet Union, Stalin rallied all of those forces which he had formerly persecuted, and an Anti-Fascist Jewish Committee was established to organize Jewish resistance to the Germans and to focus the attention of Yiddish literature on the Nazi threat.

The worst was yet to come. After the war, the Soviet regime, under the direction of the cultural czar Zhdanov, began a campaign that matched the Nazis for ruthlessness. It was directed against all manifestations of "nationalism" in literature, and Yiddish, with its esoteric language and exclusive audience, was a prime target. Early in 1948 a campaign began which resulted in the total banishment of Yiddish as a literary language. All publication in Yiddish ceased, all writers of Yiddish were sent to camps no different in the end result from the Nazi concentration camps. Yiddish writers such as Der Nister died in prison, and others, David Bergelson among them, were executed in August 1952.

After Stalin's death, there was a gradual easing of the repression. A Yiddish journal, *Sovetish Heymland* (*Soviet Homeland*), was permitted to publish articles that were supportive of the regime, but at least it was an acknowledgment that Yiddish was still a living language. In fact, in the mid-1960s modest Yiddish editions of Sholom Aleichem's works began appearing. But, as Irving Howe says, "an odor of death lingers over Yiddish in the Soviet Union. What Hitler had left undone, Stalin completed."

The Great Shtetl in America

Between 1881 and 1922, when the first immigrant quota was set, over two million East European Jews came to the United States, and the vast majority of them settled initially on the Lower East Side of New York. The Jews represented the second largest group of immigrants to come to these shores; only Italians came in greater numbers, and they too settled into the same part of Manhattan Island. Little Italy and Little Israel, as they were called, recreated, only on a larger scale, life in the old country for millions of Jews and Italians. They shared poverty, hope, despair, and adventure, and brought to America the voice of immigrant cultures that had not yet been heard here.

Of course there had been Jews in America before. Some authorities point to a Jewish presence in Virginia in 1621, and in Massachusetts by 1649. We are certain that a shipload of Jewish Sephardim had made their way to New Amsterdam in the 1650s, and, in spite of Peter Stuyvesant's inhospitable welcome, were permitted to settle. By 1733, with the arrival of Jews in Georgia, they could be found in every one of the thirteen colonies. The earliest Sephardim were in the majority until around 1750, when German Jews began to outnumber them. By the end of the war of 1812, there were about ten thousand Jews in the United States. The first synagogue was not established until 1730, indicating that there was no great religious hold on them. They blended in almost immediately with the Christian majority, and, because the American colonists really held to the idea of separation of church and state, from the beginning the Jews felt no governmental restrictions or limitations. The colonial Jew dressed like everyone else, lived where he pleased, and was indistinguishable from his fellow Americans.

The first large wave of Jewish immigration took place during the political upheavals in Europe which started with the Napoleonic era. German Jews in particular joined the millions of other political refugees who sought to escape the warring armies by fleeing to America. Again, they found in America that astonishing opportunity and freedom which they had not experienced in Europe for centuries. Jewish settlers took full advantage of the opportunities which the Louisiana Purchase offered and moved away from the eastern cities to the South and West, where they joined with non-Jewish German groups in an easy and generally harmonious association. In Cincinnati, Louisville, St. Louis, and many other cities of the Midwest, all German-speaking people joined together in *Turnvereine* (athletic clubs) and *Sangvereine* (singing clubs). Once again, it was quite convenient for the Jews to give up whatever association they had with traditional Judaism, and the swelling numbers of German Jews of a Reform background made no great effort to establish a strong Jewish religious or intellectual tradition in America. They wanted opportunity, and they found it.

By the outbreak of the Civil War there were nearly two hundred thousand Jews in the United States, and they participated fully in the conflict. Jews had settled in the South and were involved in the tobacco industry in South Carolina and Georgia. They were no less patriotic than their fellow Jews in Boston and New York and threw themselves with considerable energy into the fighting and ideological conflict. Judah Benjamin was Secretary of State of the Confederacy under Jefferson Davis.

After the war, all the hard work and diligence of the German Jews paid off handsomely. Fortunes were to be made, and the German Jews found the path to wealth most accessible to them in retail trade. Taking full advantage of the free enterprise system and the farming boom, these entrepreneurs began peddling ready-made goods to the land-owning families that could not get to the city to shop. Jewish peddlers labored long hours on the American roads, trading with grateful housewives who otherwise might never see a skirt or a mirror. Eventually, the Jewish peddlers became the great retailing families of America, headquartered particularly in New York City. These were the families that comprised "Our Crowd," the great German-Jewish alliances made among names such as Straus, Warburg, Seligman, Rosenwald, Schiff, and Guggenheim.[6] In terms of Jewish identity, this was a remarkable society. Almost strictly oriented toward Reform Judaism, the group emulated in every way it could the values and successes of the Gentile wealthy around them. They bought the same houses in the same architectural style, attempted to vacation at the same places (if subtle anti-Jewish exclusions did not keep them out), and in general imitated the style of life of the non-Jewish rich. Some felt it was silly to maintain any relationship with the Jewish past in this land of opportunity. For instance, one young man, August Schoenberg, decided to give up any relationship to his faith; by taking the French equivalent of his name, "beautiful mountain," he became August Belmont. He converted to Christianity and became one of the leading social figures of New York society.

This was the picture of American Jewry on the eve of the greatest social revolution in the nation's history. Economically, America's Jews had established themselves securely in the American Dream. Most had moved into the middle class, and others had attained a level of wealth unthinkable except in dreams of the Rothschilds. Jewish philanthropy was considerable already; America did indeed seem to represent the Promised Land. Finally, the Jew could move with total freedom—and anonymity—among the peoples of a nation. The German-Jewish American had indeed become an American, in terms of culture, language, attitude, and allegiance.

It was this total absorption into the American way of life which made the events of the decade of 1880 all the more traumatic for these people, as they looked with disbelief at the wretched masses of Russian Jews pouring into lower Manhattan, Jews who looked to the uptown Jews for aid and assistance because after all, they thought, a Jew is a Jew. But the gap that separated the German Jews from the Hassidic Russian Jews was enormous, and at first the established Jewish community recoiled with horror at the sight of these miserable masses. Organizations were established and sent to Europe, to urge these displaced people to look elsewhere for a homeland: America could not absorb them. Considerable Jewish energy was consumed in attempts to stop the wave of immigration, but it was in vain. Eventually, the Jewish establishment threw itself into the struggle to improve the situation of the downtown Jews. Emma Lazarus, Lillian Wald, and many other good-willed people of wealth established settlement houses to clean and educate the ghetto children and to fight for legislation to improve slum life for both Jews and

Gentiles who were living in what has been described as America's biggest slum.

A reporter for the *New York Tribune,* writing in the September 15, 1898 issue, described his visit to Orchard Street, the heart of the Jewish Lower East Side:

> The neighborhood where these people live is absolutely impassable for wheeled vehicles other than their pushcarts. If a truckdriver tries to get through where their pushcarts are standing they apply to him all kinds of vile and indecent epithets. The driver is fortunate if he gets out of the street without being hit with a stone or having a putrid fish thrown in his face. This neighborhood, peopled almost entirely by people who claim to have been driven from Russia and Poland, is the eyesore of New York and perhaps the filthiest place on the western continent. It is impossible for a Christian to live there because he will be driven out, either by blows or the dirt and stench. Cleanliness is an unknown quantity to these people. They cannot be lifted up to a higher plane because they do not want to be.

Similar descriptions of Italian, Greek, and, some years earlier, Irish neighborhoods, filled the newspapers of American cities. The hordes of immigrants, packed into decaying neighborhoods, living on the average of ten to a room in cold-water tenements without toilets, lived and died the life of the urban ghetto dweller of any age, any generation. The Jews on the Lower East Side of New York were no different, and from the beginning of the 1880s, they experienced the same harsh treatment and deprivations which ghetto dwellers at all times experience. The environment was hostile, and during the first years of mass immigration, thousands of desperate men and women died in the struggle for existence.[7] Death, disease, crime, and exploitation were the commonly shared backgrounds for all those who found themselves locked into the teeming ghetto.

Yet in spite of all the deprivation, it was different, and it was better than any *shtetl*—because, for five cents, the miserable immigrant could buy himself a subway ride to any place in the vast expanse of New York City. He was free to wander, free to go anywhere he wished. It was this freedom which was ultimately to change even the horrors of the ghetto.

As one might guess from the reporter's piece in the *New York Tribune,* the immigrant neighborhoods were not looked upon too kindly by the upper social classes. The neighborhoods of immigrant Jews were no different, although the great tradition of education in the *shtetl* did encourage them to take every advantage which the city government offered them. Jews flocked into the public schools of the lower Manhattan district, where they found that 80 percent of their teachers were members of another ethnic group, the one which had preceded the Jews in their current neighborhood, the Irish. The street names of the Lower East Side were hardly Jewish: Ludlow, Rivington, Orchard, Delancey, Essex, Hester, Stanton. The Irish had helped name them forty years earlier when, driven to America by the potato famine in Ireland, they occupied the tenements. But the Irish had come a long way; they now were a powerful force in politics and education. The Irish school teacher was a model for the Jewish immigrant mother, who could barely speak English herself but who could appreciate the mellifluous sounds of English, especially when spoken with an Irish accent. From the very outset it was this opportunity of a free education, indeed *compulsory* education, which proved to be the key to the opportunities in the new world. For some, the *shtetl* in America, no matter how poor, was a comfortable place to live because it was familiar. To others, however, the main idea in their lives was *to escape,* to break out of this ghetto, to make it in America.

From the very start, one inevitably found those same activities which the poor gravitate to in the hopes of finding the Golden Road. Amidst the endless pushcarts, selling everything from shoelaces to bagels, there was the breeding ground for criminals, showmen, scholars, and prizefighters. Soon there were Jewish children born of immigrant parents, but this was a new kind of Jewish youth, called Moishe at home, but Mickey or Michael at school, not satisfied with the world of his parents, determined to strike it rich. Often the parents had laid the groundwork. The greatest single employer on the Lower East Side was the newly developing ready-to-wear garment industry, which employed thousands of newly arrived immigrants in sweatshops, and permitted little children to take work home for additional pennies in the family coffers. The inhuman working conditions strengthened the workers' natural inclination toward labor organizations, which had begun in Europe, and the next step was the formation of unions, made up of Jews, Italians, Polish and Russian immigrants. The International Ladies' Garment Workers' Union was founded in 1900, to be followed by the Fur Workers' Union and the Cap Makers' Union in 1901 and 1904. With the establishment of the Amalgamated Clothing Workers' Union in 1914, trade unionism as an immigrant phenomenon could not be ignored in New York City. From 1909 to 1914 strikes occurred regularly, and the industry faced the workers in a grim confrontation of willpower. Tragedy was never far away, and the worst one took place in 1911, when the sweatshop Triangle Shirtwaist Factory burned down, trapping 143 young girls, who perished. Those who died in the flames were the children of the immigrants, and out of their human sacrifice came new child labor laws and better working conditions for the ghetto. This was not a confrontation of Jew and Gentile, for many of the sweatshops were owned by Jews, from uptown and elsewhere. The contribution of these immigrant unions to the labor movement in America was enormous, and for decades to come organized labor in the United States was identified with these Jewish, Italian, and Irish founders.

At the same time, other young Jews found their way into less idealistic activities. Jewish prostitution was a documented fact, and Allen Street was the Red Light district. The Jew who was impatient with the opportunities in education and labor turned to crime, and participated fully in all the criminal activities of the underworld. After centuries of passivity in the Diaspora, one of the unwanted benefits of freedom was a new inclination toward violence. When Murder, Inc. was a flourishing organization in the 1920s, it was made up almost exclusively of Jewish "hit men." Names such as Abe Relas, Louis (Buchhalter) Lepke, Arnold Rothstein, Ben "Bugsy" Siegel, and Meyer Lansky gave the Lower East Side of New York both a Jewish as well as an underworld flavor. Rothstein, it was alleged, had been the key operative in the fixing of the 1919 World Series.[8]

Above all, there was a vitality, a fierce energy which dominated life in the ghetto. After centuries of restriction and censorship, the Jew could walk, as Abba Shuster's son Gimpel had said, with his eyes off the ground. He could also read, write, and speak freely, and the Jews took full advantage of this opportunity to create one of the great immigrant cultures of America, in an immigrant language, Yiddish. Theatres producing outrageous melodrama as well as a Yiddish *King Lear* were packed with Jews eager and hungry for any kind of entertainment (*Lear* was a standard offering, close to the Jewish heart, with "rotten" daughters not taking care of the aged father).

Literally every adult Jew read a Yiddish newspaper. In the peak years of the 1920s, the circulation of the Yiddish daily press in New York City alone was nearly seven hundred thousand, and conservative estimates suggested that each paper was read by three adults, accounting for a readership of over two million people. More than any other institution, the Jewish press reflected the sense of expanding freedom which the Jews enjoyed in America. In Czarist Russia publication of papers for the Jewish masses was strictly controlled, and, given the opportunity in America, they proliferated in order to appeal to every possible political and ideological shade of opinion. The Jew revelled in his freedom, and his choice of reading material reflected this newly discovered sense of expansiveness. The first daily newspaper was the *Tageblatt,* established in 1885. After that, a succession of papers appeared, each one identified with some religious or political inclination. The *Morgen Journal,* begun in 1901, became the voice of orthodoxy and political conservatism. It generally supported Republicans in American political campaigns and ran counter to the socialist-liberal trend on the East Side. Politically and intellectually opposite was *Die Varheit (Truth),* also founded in 1901 and edited by a prominent Jewish intellectual, Louis Miller. *Die Varheit* and later *Der Tog (The Day)* appealed to the secular Jews who had fallen away from religion and Jewish orthodoxy. It was liberal, reformed, enlightened. It was also committed to a nonsocialist political ideology.

By far the most important and influential daily was the *Jewish Daily Forward (Forverts),* established in 1897 and edited from 1902 until 1951 by the most prominent figure in immigrant journalism in this country, Abraham Cahan. Cahan had trained as an English-speaking journalist, had studied the techniques of marketing, of the Lincoln Steffens brand of muckraking and investigatory crusading, and was prepared to revolutionize the Yiddish press in America. The *Forward* under Cahan took up the cause of trade unionism, attacked the sweatshops and slum conditions—in short, became the voice for Jewish socialism in America. Cahan made strong editorial policy, would advocate strikes, and he was in no small measure responsible for the fact that the Jewish labor movement in the United States remained safely in the camp of Social Democracy and never swung over to radicalism. Cahan was a firm believer in the American Dream for the Jew, and he did not like any of the more dramatic solutions which Bolsheviks, and later Trotskyite or Stalinist groups, urged on the immigrant community. He was often accused of softness by the more revolutionary groups within the American *shtetl,* but his newspaper never swayed from the political course he had selected. At its peak the *Forward*'s circulation was over two hundred and fifty thousand copies daily.

Yiddish Literature in America

Above all, Cahan understood circulation and readership psychology. He appreciated the fact that women in America would read a Yiddish newspaper as well. He added features, columns, and even literature which appealed particularly to the Yiddish public in America. Cahan changed the face of Jewish journalism, and provided an opportunity for Yiddish writers to reach an audience concentrated in one area. The *Forward* encouraged young writers to submit stories, and soon every Yiddish paper in New York was publishing fiction and poetry, still written in Yiddish but now very specifically addressing the problems of life in America. Old habits were not easily broken. There was still, as in the time of Sholom Aleichem and Peretz (both of whom were still alive in 1914), an intimacy between reader and author which one rarely encountered in literatures with which we are more familiar. The Yiddish writer traditionally wrote about a world and an experience which were commonly shared. In the literature of the Lower East Side, the Jew was no longer concerned with Czarist oppression, pogroms, or quotas for Jews in school. This was all part of the past. There were new problems, new preoccupations, and, ironically, new threats just as disturbing as those in the old world.

One means of keeping in touch with the interests and problems of the reader was again attributable to an Abraham Cahan innovation. Cahan always believed that the readers had a great deal on their minds which they would like to see in print. So, in the January 20, 1906 issue he published three letters from readers who had written personally to him to ask for advice and to talk about their *tzures*, their problems. He published these letters in a column called *A Bintel Brief*, a bundle of letters. The feature became an enormous success overnight. The Jewish immigrant daily poured out his heart to Abe Cahan in sacks of mail, and Cahan would try to personally answer as many as he possibly could, until the task became overwhelming. In his memoirs, which he wrote in 1929, Cahan wrote of the *Bintel Brief*:

> People often need the opportunity to be able to pour out their heavy-laden hearts. Among our immigrant masses this need was very marked. Hundreds of thousands of people, torn from their homes and their dear ones, were lonely souls who thirsted for expression, who wanted to hear an opinion, who wanted advice in solving their weighty problems. The *Bintel Brief* created just this opportunity for them.

The problems revealed in the *Bintel Brief* letters provided a vast resource of materials for the Yiddish writers now looking for themes of interest. Inevitably, certain preoccupations remained constant, regardless of whether the setting was the old world or the new: *yichus, naches,* respect, *parnosseh, mishpoche.* There were rich men in both worlds, greed and envy, heartache and troubles.

There were also new problems, ones which were only understood in terms of the crisis in Czarist Russia, as one generation of Jewish youth attempted to escape the restrictions of traditional *shtetl* ways. For Jewish youth in America presented a threat to tradition which was even more devastating

than that which Hodel or Chava presented to Tevye. Invari-
ably, the audience seeing Tevye's tragedy could look to their
own family and see that, thank God, it could not happen to
them. But in America anything was possible. The Jew was no
longer a prisoner in the *shtetl*. The opportunities to meet
Gentile children were infinitely greater, the occasions to
leave the *shtetl* environment infinitely more frequent. For the
old-world Jewish parent, there was at least one positive side
to the misery of the *shtetl*: your children were secure within
your family life. In New York's Lower East Side, this was not
the case. As soon as the generation born in America after the
First World War began to think beyond the borders of the
Lower East Side, they took full advantage of their geographic
mobility. Singer's "The Little Shoemakers" avoids the generational conflict in these terms, because the children of Abba
had already moved to suburbia when he arrived in America.
But in the first decade of the twentieth century the Delancey
Street and Williamsburg bridges, which united the Lower
East Side with Brooklyn and Long Island, were constructed.
The potential for genuine family crises was great; the American Jew, by the 1920s, consisted of two distinct generations,
one old and traditional, the other younger, ambitious and
eager to explore. One was rooted in Yiddish, the other in
English.

It was to the older generation that the Yiddish writers in
America responded, it was to them that the Yiddish newspapers directed their fiction, and the literature clearly reflected the interests of that population. "The Little Shoemakers" is intended to offer a soothing and mollifying solution
to the problem of aging of the older generation of Jews in
America. Sholem Asch, with his customary directness, presents the other side of the coin, the grim, dark image of the
disintegration of the Jewish family as seen from the American side; Singer in his sentimental tale tries to suggest that
the American experience has united families as they were

not united even in Frampol; Asch dramatizes the disturbing effect of success on children. In "A Quiet Garden Spot" he sketches for his East Side audience a picture of what might happen to them. Asch's Jewish family is particularly pathetic, a lost old couple living in a quiet and desperate isolation, ignored by their two grown sons, who are preoccupied with their own ambitions. The brothers, Notteh and Anshel, don't even see each other, they accidentally meet on occasion, but all feeling of family identity is gone. The old couple spend their lonely evenings under the dim kitchen light, reminiscing about what ironically have become "the good old days." The infrequent visits from their sons are marked by a leit-motif, repeated several times in the brief sketch: "Don't worry, we'll take good care of you." But little Shimmon continues working in the factory in Brooklyn until he dies of exhaustion. At the grave, the sons once again promise: "Don't worry, we'll take good care of you, Ma." The life of the widowed old lady was one that the Lower East Side residents dreaded:

After the funeral the sons vied with each other for the honor of having their mother during the seven days of mourning. She went to stay with her elder son, a salesman, who was more prosperous. The following week she spent with her younger son. And thus she wandered back and forth like a nomad, staying now with one son, now with the other, until her benefactors decided to place her in a home for the aged.

And Asch articulates the most feared and frightening fate for the Jewish parent in America, a fate which was never articulated in Yiddish literature in Europe because it simply was not a problem. In America, the threat of the old age home had become a reality, as the Jewish aged were not able to adjust to the lives of the next generation. But before the sons could put the old woman away, she died. Again Asch contrasts old world customs with new world developments. In the *shtetl* the family burial plot was as traditional a part of life as it was of death. The *shtetl* cemetery, the burial society, the knitting of shrouds, the preparation of grave sites, these were given the utmost, serious attention. In Asch's story the old couple cannot even be buried side by side. "The grave next to him now belonged to a stranger.... She was buried in a remote and neglected part of the cemetery. Thus were the old folks parted in death: he was interred among strangers in one place, while she had to rest among strange women in another." Then, as if by a miracle, the two grave sites were transformed into flower gardens by wind-blown seeds. Years later—the brothers had not seen each other— one of them goes to the cemetery for the burial of a lodge brother ("He would have been fined had he failed to appear") and remembers that this is the graveyard of his parents. The son is awestruck and amazed to discover the beautiful flowers growing on the graves. Nature had filled the vacuum left by the children.

Asch's story is deliberately overdrawn. His purpose is to show the Jewish elderly—the younger Jews were not even reading such stories in Yiddish any longer—what they might have to look forward to. It is a grim picture of alienation, of the thanklessness of rearing children, and particularly of the dangers which American life hold for the aging Jew. Asch remembers that in the *shtetl* such a fate would not be expected. Singer's "Little Shoemakers" and Asch's "Quiet Garden Spot" represent the type of story which throws a nostalgic look at *shtetl* life, as the anxieties of the American experience begin to filter into Jewish sensibility.

Even the enormous economic opportunities which America offered could be fraught with danger for the Jews. The *nogid* in America was exposed to wealth which he could not dream of in the *shtetl*, but he was suspected of having to pay too high a price for his gains. Pesach Marcus (1896–1973) wrote his sketch "Higher and Higher" for the Yiddish press to make this point. It is the tale of an American *nogid,* the price of success, and a moralistic statement to the Jew not to lose his soul for money, which, ironically, "could only happen in America." The *shtetl nogid,* even the Menachem Mendel-like *luftmensh,* was never far from God; he considered himself a business partner of the Almighty, and any good fortune that should come his way was directly attributable to divine intervention. Not so with Harry Cooper, "a little man with short flabby legs, whose belly swelled like a bladder," a Jewish real estate speculator in New York determined to make himself into something. Harry Cooper is driven by the quest for success, he stomps on former friends in order to climb to the top, he races from tenement to tenement, collecting his rents. "Harry kept climbing and climbing, and his belly grew bigger and bigger." Harry is a slumlord, with houses in Harlem and the Lower East Side, but he is not satisfied and enters into a deal for a high-priced luxury apartment house, the House of Tomorrow, with a bank run by Gentiles. His financial dealings with the bank are primarily with a bizarre little character. "He pirouetted around the office, and his nails were painted. He had a voice like a bird's, and his name was Van Sickel." [9] But Cooper is not clever enough, and he loses his controlling interest in the high-rise, all his assets disappear, and Van Sickel has him at his mercy. Van Sickel tells Cooper that he wants him around just to make certain that no Jews attempt to rent:

> Mr. Cooper, the House of Tomorrow will pay only if high society moves in here. We must not open to anyone who can pay rent. Former rag collectors, all those Levines, Goldsteins, and their ilk—don't misunderstand me, Mr. Cooper, I personally have nothing against them. But not everyone can stand their manners.... After all, we must not expect a Social Register family to live in the same house with immigrants. In fact, Mr. Cooper, you can be very helpful. Jews are very clever, they often assume Irish

or other non-Jewish names, but you, Mr. Cooper, can recognize another one under any disguise.

Cooper finally realizes that he has been turned into an enemy of his own people. He remembers his poor relatives and friends on Orchard Street, who are "surprised by the visit of this millionaire who owned a great palace and had for so many years ignored them." Harry wants to take them to the House of Tomorrow, and a truckload of people from Orchard Street, with nothing else to do on a hot summer night, ride uptown, to discover the entrance barred by Van Sickel and the staff. Cooper gets his revenge, however, by diving to his death from the top of the tower. His spilled blood on the marble entrance in part pays for the sins he committed against his people.

Marcus's story clearly is directed at his New York *shtetl* audience. The relationship with the Gentile world of banking which Cooper indulges in is a direct warning: now that we are free to have business dealings with the *goyim*, remember that they are ten times smarter than the Jews! Stay with your own kind, be happy with what you have, and don't think you're such a big deal.... In Marcus's little morality tale, emancipation and opportunity brought only death to Harry Cooper. He had forgotten all that was important: family, friends, kinship, religion, loyalty to the past, in favor of the American dream of wealth.

Increasingly, one encountered the themes of nostalgia for the old world in Yiddish culture in America. The threat of emancipation and assimilation was beginning to overwhelm the Jewish immigrant, whose children were now more often than not living miles away, in New Jersey or Long Island. The *Bintel Brief* letters in the decades of the 1920s and 1930s continued to harp on the theme of the alienation of the older generation. Besides reading the newspapers, the largest Yiddish-speaking audience in the United States could be found listening on Sundays to New York radio station WEVD, which presented Yiddish-language programming for twelve hours. Two of these hours were regularly assigned to what might be called radio drama. Actually, it was Jewish soap opera, stories which captured the imagination of the radio public. Hardly a week would go by without one of the dramas focusing on the theme of aging, of a parent being forced into a home for old people; or any variation, such as in "A Quiet Garden Spot," in which the parents or grandparents are shuttled between children who have neither time for nor interest in them.

Naturally there was also relief from these anxieties, and the writers provided it as well. Joseph Opatoshu's (1887–1954) narrative, "The Eternal Wedding Gown," initially written for a newspaper but later dramatized as a radio play, artfully combines the themes of death and *naches,* of the inevitable passing of the older generation and the perfect image of children doing their duty and fulfilling their obligations to the parents. It is also a story of tradition, indeed of orthodoxy and the old ways, of keeping faith in America.

Gliche Schreiber is an eighty-year-old woman who has just returned from the funeral of her cousin Ernestine, who, when she turned from orthodox Judaism to Reform, changed her name from Gliche. "She had gone over to the reformed synagogue all of fifty years ago. Ernestine's angel (since every human being has an angel up in heaven) had turned a deaf ear to her ever since. He had never heard her pleas, since she has strayed so early from the path of true Jewishness." Gliche had given Ernestine her own shroud, her burial garment, because one had been lacking, and now it was time to make another. But this is not a story of the Lower East Side. Gliche Schreiber lives in a magnificent apartment overlooking Central Park which her two sons had provided for her. In a moment of contemplation, her eyes fall on the table covered with family photographs, mostly older relatives from Europe:

Gliche felt a glow at the sight of them. Nor was it Gliche alone who delighted in these forebears. Her two sons, doctors both, who refrained from writing on the Sabbath, as well as her son-in-law, a wealthy manufacturer who kept his shop closed on that day, also rejoiced in these ancestors. Every Sabbath eve one of her grandsons would drop in on Gliche to pronounce the benediction over the Sabbath wine. The grandson would sleep over and escort her next morning to the synagogue. For that matter, what about her sons and her son-in-law? Why, they would be welcomed in Paradise if only for the way they honored their mother (even her son-in-law called her that).

Opatoshu provides here for the less fortunate but perhaps hopeful Jewish mother a perfect image of *naches*, getting a full measure of satisfaction from one's children and grandchildren. There is a commitment to orthodoxy, to tradition, to honoring the family, and particularly to honoring the mother. *Yichus* appears in abundance, what with the fulfillment of every Jewish mother's dream of having two sons be doctors!

Opatoshu is not satisfied, though, simply to provide an escapist fairytale. Gliche's elderly friends surprise her with a visit, and bring with them their knitting: they will make her a new shroud, to replace the one she gave to Ernestine. Lurking not far away is death: "The old women threaded their needles with long white threads. And as they bent over, sewing the eternal wedding gown, death began to spin its web."

There is one other interesting dimension to *yichus* and well-being in America which emerges in this story, as it did in "The Little Shoemakers," as a measure of upward economic mobility for the Jew, and that is the figure of the black servant. More than any other ethnic group, Jews became associated with the black servant almost as soon as they were able to establish themselves beyond the minimal economic level. The more they approached middle-class respectability, the more frequently one encountered the image of the *shvartze* in Yiddish writings. In Opatoshu's story, she even speaks, of course in Yiddish, and the writer makes an ingenuous effort to have the black maid Elizabeth speak a kind of "black" Yiddish dialect.

Yet it remained for Sholom Aleichem to be the definitive chronicler of the Jew in America in that immigrant world. Although he died in 1916, he could see the potential, the irreversible movement of life for the Jew in the American ghetto. In his own few years in America he was astonished at the educational opportunities which were open to immigrants. When he came to this country, he was cheered by enormous crowds who came to Cooper Union College to listen to his lectures. His plays were produced in Yiddish in this country before they ever had a production in Europe. For Sholom Aleichem it was clear that America was to be the new home for the Jewish *shtetl*, and that the impact of America would be enormous. He had chosen his figure to represent this change in his writings. Tevye was appropriate for the old world, but for measuring the experience in a dynamic America, he needed someone younger, more flexible, more able to adapt to these exciting times. He selected a young orphan boy, Mottel, and took him on a journey from Kasrilevke, the *shtetl* of Sholom Aleichem's Old-World fiction, to a tenement on Rivington Street in New York. In *The Adventures of Mottel the Cantor's Son* we have the most complete chronicle of the grand journey, told with Sholom Aleichem's detachment and good humor, but above all with the accuracy and irony of Yiddish literature's most remarkable social historian. The "Mottel in America" segments of this book-length series of adventures take the reader into the midst of the ghetto after poignantly describing the arrival at Ellis Island, the separations and reunions. It is a world of pushcarts, penny sodas, seeing Charlie Chaplin for the first time, and strikes. Everyone has two names, a Yiddish one used by his parents, another in English for the streets and friends. Sholom Aleichem's Mottel is a boy growing up on the sidewalks of the Lower East Side.

What are those streets like today? One thing is for certain, they are still there. And if one has the time, on a Sunday, one can return to those memories and discover that, at least superficially, things look much the same. There are still mobs of people walking the streets, the same tenement buildings that were filled with immigrants still stand on Ludlow, Rivington, Orchard, and Stanton. One will still see an occasional Hassid, with long coat, beard and black, broad-brimmed hat, shouting at a passer-by. But the streets are likely to be filled with suburban tourists, out-of-towners, some blacks, and the largely local Puerto Rican population, and the Hassid's shouts might sound something like *Amigele, Amigele, kim areyn und koyf a poor zapatas,* a delightful mixture of Yiddish and Spanish urging the potential buyer to come in and purchase a pair of shoes. The brightly painted signs over the stores are in English, the streets are empty of pushcarts and have been swept clean of debris. What is remarkable is that the neighborhood has retained as much of its old character as it has. Very few of the Jewish salespeople on the streets now actually live in the tenements above the stores. They have long since made the trek to Long Island or New Jersey, and they commute to their businesses, which had started as no more than a pushcart operated by an immigrant grandfather perhaps seventy years earlier. There are still immigrants living and working on the Lower East Side today, but they are operating *carnecerias,* Spanish butcher shops, where once kosher meat was sold. The synagogues are boarded up, the language of the streets is no longer Yiddish. The Second Avenue Yiddish Theatre is now a parking garage, the newspaper sold on the corner of Essex and Houston is *El Diario.* After a very brief historical moment, the teeming Yiddish-speaking world of the Lower East Side of New York had disappeared.

7

From Shtetl to Suburbia

IT is no difficult task to discover what happened to the world of Yiddishkeit which was so alive as late as the 1930s, even after the flow of immigration was cut off by the restrictive laws passed by Congress after 1922. Whether it was the sensational Sacco-Vanzetti case or the general fear of the impact that millions of European immigrants were having on the American life style, the mood of America turned ugly and racist. The immigrant was considered by many reputable academic sociologists as no more than "the alien in our midst."[1] Actually, many of the second-generation children of these immigrants, that is, the first American-born children, would tend to agree with the description. Never was a group so thoroughly taken with the potential of the American Dream. The child of the European immigrant had successfully overcome the most important obstacles which could hinder his achieving all that he wanted. Primarily, there was language. This was not a speaker of Yiddish or Italian, but a native-born American who had heard a foreign language as a child, and for whom the *mama-loschen* was no more than a secret code used by his parents to communicate thoughts which they wished to keep from their children. It was this generation which made the explosive leap out of the American *shtetl* into the American melting pot. Educated in the New York City public school system, it had available to it the enormous higher educational resources of a system which offered in effect a free college education. Brooklyn College, Hunter, the City College of New York (CCNY), and Queens College became almost the exclusive training grounds for New York's children of the immigrants. At one point in the 1930s, Brooklyn College was over 90 percent Jewish in ethnic background. The schools regularly closed on the Jewish holidays. With some frequency the genuinely adventurous young man or woman would step outside the traditional educational pattern of the commuter to the city campus and attend New York City's Ivy League school, Columbia University, or the equally prestigious private New York University (NYU). Within the traditional *shtetl* matrix, once again the Jewish family was dealing with aspects of *yichus*—the status acquired by attending a school other than the "regular" city institutions. But *real* status meant leaving the city and the urban commuting life and attending a college out of town. For the Jew this usually meant Cornell University in upstate Ithaca, since the New York City Regents' Scholarships applied in part to that Ivy League school and ghetto students could manage the expense if there were sufficient funds available to live away. Jewish parents were willing to make any required sacrifice, no matter how great, to send their children to the best and most prestigious school possible, so much so that the number of Jewish students in attendance at Columbia and even Harvard, became a matter of concern to those institutions, both of which were caught up in the antiimmigrant spirit of the times. As Irving Howe has pointed out, Harvard issued a formal statement in 1922 suggesting that a review be made concerning the number of Jewish students in attendance at Harvard.[2] President Abbott Lowell considered the state of affairs a definite problem for Harvard; the other prestigious Ivy League institutions, including the Seven-Sister group of women's colleges, had instituted quotas on the number of Jewish students who might attend their universities and colleges by the end of the 1920s.[3]

But no quota system, no social restrictions or exclusions could keep the sons and daughters of the immigrants from participating in the American Dream. They insisted on their rights to become as thoroughly Americanized as possible, they fled in great numbers from identification with the world of their parents. They challenged real estate limitations, university quotas, blackballing in country clubs. They merely asked the established society what it would require to gain admission, and often enough the answer was acceptable to them: blend in, become as American as we are. As they pushed their way into the formerly Gentile suburbs all over America, this did not seem a particularly high price to pay. One could still, they felt, maintain a sense of Jewish identity, even if the local synagogue looked like a church, had a huge parking lot, and conducted a service that took into account the fact that the world had changed from Kasrilevke and the Lower East Side of New York.

The urge to belong, the drive to become part of, this was the overwhelming force behind the generation of Jewish Americans growing up in pre-World War II America. Orthodoxy was on the decline, and the American Reform Judaism movement was the fastest growing of the three branches of Judaism.[4] In one brief moment, it seemed, a generation of Mottels and Moishes had become Meyers and Miltons, and were now, as the *children* of the American-born son or daughter of an immigrant family walking the tree-lined streets of suburbia, Kevin and Debbie.

Perhaps the most leveling experience of all was the Second World War. The idea of *being a part* was thoroughly ingrained in the American mind. Americans of all ethnic backgrounds were joined against the common enemies. Hollywood's idea of the melting pot theory of assimilation was repeated in almost every war movie. No fighting unit was complete without an Italian, an Irishman, a Jew, and "a kid from the midwest." Brooklyn—by this time the two great bridges had permitted the immigrants to swarm into Williamsburg and Greenpoint—was guaranteed to produce a chuckle and a recognizable ghetto dialect. The war, in effect, made everyone "equal," and the many formidable social barriers to assimilation and to equal opportunities fell away. When the young Americans returned from Europe and the Pacific, they were eager to make up for lost economic opportunities and to throw themselves back into the pleasant task of "making it" in America. The G.I. Bill, G.I. Home Loans, a restrengthened sense of Americanism, all conspired to produce opportunities to move even further away, physically and spiritually, from *The World of Our Fathers*. The gaps between the American Tevyes and their children grew wider. The opportunity to blend in was so great that it seemed that America was going to be the land where the "Jewish problem" was finally going to be solved.

Even the horrors of the Holocaust and the founding of the state of Israel did remarkably little to establish a sense of Jewish consciousness in America. The destruction of six million Jews in Europe caused an initial wave of disbelief, but it fell to a small minority in the United States to articulate the meaning of the Holocaust; the majority of American Jews were immediately caught up in the quest for *parnosseh* and the continued dream which the war had interrupted: the casting off of Jewish identity in favor of an American consciousness. Both the idea of a Jewish state and the singling out of the Jews for destruction by the Nazis represented an unwished-for interference, and most Jews simply pushed these Jewish consciousness-raising thoughts out of their minds, in order to get on with the more practical and pleasant task of becoming a fully integrated American.

Along with the Jewish identity, the Jewish neighborhood disappeared or changed color. The Lower East Side of New York, Roxbury and Dorchester in Boston, Chicago's North Side, the old neighborhoods of Philadelphia and Milwaukee, all sent the Jews out into the tree-lined streets of suburbia and replaced them in the tenements with blacks and Puerto Ricans. Those symbols and signs of the ghetto inhabitant altered to suit the new population. The boxing champions were no longer Kaplan, Rosenbloom, Rosenberg, and Baer. Sugar Ray Robinson and Joe Louis, more than any other American figures, heralded the change by defeating representatives from every ethnic group in the United States in their climb to the world championships of their divisions. Louis particularly, in the 1930s, took on white ethnic America: Abe Simon, Lou Novikoff, Max and "Buddy" Baer, Tony Galento, "Irish" Billy Conn, Tami Mauriello and a host of others.[5] In Robinson's classic struggles with Graziano and La Motta in the late '40s and early '50s, one might find the last hegemony of the white man in professional boxing.

The Continuity of Tradition

We are at the point in this narrative when we might be prepared to accept the complete disappearance of Jewish life in America. The last generation of native-speaking Yiddish Old-World Jews was growing old; their children were finding relatively easy access to the golden promise of America. Jewish writers in America, and particularly Jewish scholars who were the first of the generation to *make it* academically in the '30s and '40s, showed a marked proclivity for avoiding any connection with the past. Indeed, in the academic world, it was the Jewish-American academician who seemed drawn to those writers whose view of America was one unmarred by mass immigration: Eliot, Henry James, and Ezra Pound. Above all, American literature did not offer its writers traditions which connected it in any way with the tensions or problems of what must seem the most distant of alien worlds, the East European *shtetl* familiar to Tevye, for example.

147

Therefore, one might expect that if these sons and daughters of the Jewish immigrants were going to assume their place in the development of the American literary tradition, there would be no room for any memory or reminiscence of what most of them hoped would be a tradition which, thank heavens, had died.

But they did not reckon with the extraordinary resiliency of *shtetl* values, nor with the fact that the Jew in America, no matter how assimilated or relatively at peace with himself, would carry a part of the uncertainties and travails of his past life with him wherever he went. You could take the Jew out of the *shtetl,* but, it so happened, you could not take the *shtetl* out of the Jew. After a very brief period which paralleled the temporary euphoria of full participation in American life enjoyed by the children of the immigrants, when the first-generation American writers continued the traditions of Whitman and Melville, or Hemingway and Fitzgerald, there occurred a mutation. The Jewish writer in America, just barely out of touch with his past, quickly reasserted his relationship to it. How different this was from the experience of the assimilated Jewish writer in nineteenth-century Germany who so quickly unburdened himself of his ghetto past, only to discover that the Germans were not so willing to permit him to forget.[6] In the American context, not only did the Jewish-American writer reforge the link with his origins, he also altered the forms of American writing and created themes and attitudes which until this generation were not really part of that tradition.

Perhaps it was the discovery that the American Dream would always have a good measure of insecurity associated with it for Jews, no matter how thorough the assimilation process went along, but as early as the 1940s, for example in the short stories of Delmore Schwartz, first-generation Jewish-American writers went back to the *shtetl* and its inhabitants. We discover *shlemihls, shlimmazels, luftmenshen,* and *shnor-*

rers once again, but this time placed in an American literary heritage that previously had relatively little knowledge of the "loser," of the weak, unheroic dangling man. Furthermore, these questionable types suffer from problems associated with *mishpoche*, with the family. They may have names like Tommy Wilhelm, Herzog, or Fidelman, they may wear Brooks Brothers suits, but they cannot hide the fact (their creators never try to) that they have relatives in the old country.

Thus, Yiddish literature found a home in America. Jewish literary types were able to make the transition from the *shtetl* with relative ease. The most significant event which symbolized the complete return and American metamorphosis of this literature was the appearance of Saul Bellow's *Dangling Man* in 1941. As Ruth Wisse points out in her study of *The Schlemihl as Modern Hero*,[7] Bellow was announcing to the world that something was happening in American literature. From now on, the American literary scene was going to be populated by new types, with new problems and with great uncertainties about the nature of their existence. What Bellow knew already at that time was that the *shtetl* and all its problems was making its debut in American literature. Like the Jew in the Old World, the new "heroes" of American fiction would face insecurity, doubt, family crisis, lost faith, and an uncertain future, all with the good-natured, occasionally grim good humor of travail. Where earlier the scars were physical and sometimes emotional, now, in America, where at least you could always make a living, they would be psychological and neurosis-producing.

The American spirit in literature would have to give way a bit, with its pragmatic and adventurous vision, its resourcefulness and optimistic heroism. For the Jew in America, the identity crisis brought a new dimension to his writing. What is significant is that almost immediately this crisis became his total literary preoccupation. Through this, Tevye's world has been kept alive in America.

The Awakening

The actual causes for the astonishing resurgence of Jewish consciousness in America during the mid-1950s will most likely remain a point of contention for years. Certainly it was not the sense of a large number of young writers that writing on Jewish themes in English offered a potentially great reading public. Beginning with Henry Roth's brilliant novel *Call It Sleep* (1930) and the occasional stories of S. J. Perelman and Delmore Schwartz, fiction dealing with Jewish life in America fell between the interests of two audiences. The older Yiddish readers preferred, indeed *insisted* on their literature being in the language of the old country; the new generation of assimilated Jews were simply not interested.

Bernard Malamud (1914–   ) and Philip Roth (1932–   ) appeared in the decade of the '50s, even before the enormous black literary revival; and they reached back deep into the *shtetl* heritage to rediscover the themes, the preoccupations, attitudes, even literary types of the now nearly dead world of Yiddishkeit and Yiddish literature.[8] Along with Saul Bellow (1915–   ) they represent perhaps the most concentrated source of what has been termed Jewish-American fiction.[9] This chapter will in no way attempt anything like a comprehensive study of this genre of American literature. By focusing on no more than three representative writers, we hope to underline, however, the relationship of this rebirth with the world of the *shtetl* and with the values of a folk heritage which has almost completely disappeared.

What is astonishing about much of the writings to be considered is the similarity to that which the *shtetl* world produced for an entirely different environment. The only common denominator, theoretically, which ties the old world to the new is the fact that there were Jews in both. As Roth, Malamud, and Bellow engaged the problem of Jewish identity in America, they were able, because of their proximity to that heritage, to touch those strings which would produce an

150

instantaneous reaction. At the heart of Jewish identity was, inevitably, the Jewish family. This proved to be the strongest link with the past, with the world of the East European *shtetl,* and particularly with the atmosphere of crisis which united these two seemingly different Jewish worlds. In one case, the dominant fact of existence was persecution; in the other, it was freedom. Yet they were joined by the same threat to their existence, and the literary response in each case was direct, moralistic in tone, and marked by a distinctly critical appraisal regarding the quality of Jewish life.

"Eli the Fanatic": The Crisis of Jewish Identity

Of all the writers we might identify as Jewish-American, none was as preoccupied with the disintegration of Jewish values in America as was Philip Roth. His story, "Eli the Fanatic," [10] is a genuine recasting of the style of Mendele Mocher Sforim, almost a diatribe against the generation of totally assimilated American Jews who, in the spirit of the post–World War II atmosphere of prosperity and thoughtless materialism, have almost come to the point where they have faded into the background of Protestant America and have disappeared. Here we have Philip Roth, himself not yet thirty, attempting to become the conscience of a people determined not to remember. Roth's purpose is to remind the Jew in America what it might cost *to belong.*

The small Jewish community of Woodenton, Long Island is in an uproar. For years they have struggled to gain acceptance in Woodenton, an old, established, respectable town in the suburbs. Now, in the years immediately after the end of the Second World War, they have made their peace with Woodenton and are accepted. They have given up some of "their extreme practices in order not to threaten or offend." The Jews are commuters, local businessmen, housewives, who dress and look like anyone else in town. There is no active Jewish community center or synagogue. When they have to go to *shul* or "Sunday school," they drive to another community. They have nervous breakdowns like their Gentile neighbors, paint their rocks pink like everyone else, in short, have come to be as banal and as trivial, in Roth's eyes, as suburban America can be. And the price they have paid is to represent themselves and all Jews as a pleasant, pale imitation of their non-Jewish neighbors.

This fragile paradise is disrupted by a dramatic reminder of the past. The old Puddington mansion on the outskirts of town is taken over by eighteen little Jewish boys with earlocks and a rabbi named Leo Tzuref, who has come to establish the Yeshiva of Woodenton, Long Island. Most offensive of all is the appearance of a figure in long black caftan, wide-brimmed hat, and buttoned white shirt, who also lives at the Yeshiva. He is a Hassidic assistant to Rabbi Tzuref. When the Hassid begins shopping in town, the Jews of Woodenton are outraged. They turn in their fury and desperation to one of their own, the lawyer Eli Peck, who is destined to be Roth's Jewish Everyman in a Brooks Brothers suit. The Jews of Woodenton want nothing less than the disappearance of these strangers, particularly the offending Hassid in his alien garb:

"Eli, a regular greenhorn," Ted Heller had said. "He didn't say a word. Just handed me the note and stood there, like in the Bronx the old guys who used to come around selling Hebrew trinkets...." "A Yeshiva!" Artie Berg had said. "Eli, in Woodenton, a Yeshiva! If I wanted to live in Brownsville, Eli, I'd live in Brownsville...." "Eli," Harry Shaw speaking now, "the old Puddington Place. Old man Puddington'll roll over in his grave. Eli, when I left the city, Eli, I didn't plan the city should come to me...." "Goddam fanatics," Ted said. "This is the twentieth century, Eli. Now it's the guy with the hat. Pretty soon all the little Yeshiva boys'll be spilling down into town."

Who are these strange Jews? Where did they come from? To the single-minded Jews of Woodenton, there was little room in their imaginations for the Holocaust and the destruction of European Jewry. Of all the offenses perpetrated by this band of small intruders with their two adults, none is more horrifying than the Hassid's characteristic dress. Peck is instructed to demand that the Hassid cease walking through the elegant streets of Woodenton until he has conformed sartorially, pointing out to Rabbi Tzuref that there is a Robert Hall's just down the road. Tzuref tries to communicate the meaning of the Hassid's suit:

> "To take away the one thing a man's got?"
> "Not to take away, *replace*."
> "But I tell you he has nothing. *Nothing*. You have that word in English? *Nicht? Gornisht?*"
> "Yes, Mr. Tzuref, we have the word."
> "A mother and a father?" Tzuref said. "No. A wife? No. A baby? A little ten-month-old baby? No. A village full of friends? A synagogue where you know the feel of every seat under your pants? Where with your eyes closed you could smell the cloth of the Torah? ... And a medical experiment they performed on him yet! That leaves nothing, Mr. Peck. Absolutely nothing!"
> "I misunderstood."
> "No news reached Woodenton?"

Tzuref's final question is perhaps the most telling indictment of Jewish consciousness which Roth makes in the story: "No news reached Woodenton?" means "Were the Jews of Woodenton so preoccupied with their own small world and with their efforts to forget their Jewish past that they could not spare a moment's conscience for six million Jews, no matter how ridiculous their appearance seemed to be?" And the effect on Eli Peck is significant. He above all does experience the guilt, the required remorse; he is assaulted on all sides by the tragic fate of the children and in particular of the Hassid.

But Peck is very much a product of American civilization and all that is required of an individual to survive. In the *shtetl* there was persecution, child beating, mental offenses against old and young, but the repression bred a kind of inner psychic strength. In America, there is freedom, mobility, and opportunity, but the strength which the individual drew from the community is gone, and alienation, guilt, and anxiety have replaced it. The Jew in America, like everyone else, has become a neurotic, and Eli Peck is no exception. His wife Miriam, as soon as she perceives the stress which the Yeshiva is causing her husband, suggests another session with Dr. Eckman, his therapist. She herself is also a product of the age of psychology, constantly analyzing her relationship with her unborn child, commenting on her husband's hostility, a product of what Roth describes mockingly as the New School and Freud's *Introduction to Psycho-Analysis*: the "pop" psychologist, who at the slightest provocation is prepared to give a superficial analysis of the Oedipus complex and the fetus.

There are two perceptions of Eli Peck's problem, and his response to the Hassid displays both of them. He presents the Hassid with his own best suit, hoping that modern dress will make the little DP children and their teachers acceptable to the community. However, Peck is not prepared for what happens. The Hassid appears at the Pecks' back door, and drops a package before racing off. It is the black caftan. Eli, mentally fragile, sympathetic toward the plight of these displaced Jews, in a word, vulnerable, gives himself over to his expanding sense of Judaism, assumes the responsibility of acknowledging his spiritual relationship with the children and the Hassid. He stands in front of his mirror and first places on his head the smooth-brimmed hat of the Hassid. Then he undresses, and item by item, including the fringed orthodox undergarment, he puts on the Hassid's clothes.

Driven by an all-consuming, centuries-old sense of guilt at the thought that he represents the final destruction of a world he wishes to deny, Eli Peck gives in. He admits: I am a Jew, I am a part of the world of these black threads that smell of the *shtetl;* in this spirit, he walks down the main street of Woodenton, saying "Sholom" to anyone who passes. He seems to go out of his way to underline his Jewish identity, particularly to the very people from whom he had shielded it for so many years. Up and down Coach House Road, the ultimate suburban street, with a Colonial-styled supermarket, Eli finds the president of the Lions' Club, the epitome of proper, Gentile Woodenton.

What has happened to Eli has happened inside his own world, and it makes sense to him there. To the others, Peck is merely reverting to form. He is having another nervous breakdown, for how else could one explain the embarrassing madness of his act. Miriam has in the meantime given birth to their child, and Eli rushes to the hospital. When his wife sees him in the Hassid's clothes, she, the Freudian suburban Jewish housewife, is the first to assume a mental relapse, and expresses her anguish in terms which are hostile, aggressive, and yet filled with the condescending sympathy of those assured of their own psychological well-being:

"Eli, you can't go around like that!"
"I have a son. I want to see him."
"Eli, why are you doing this to me!" Red seeped back into her lips. "*He's* not your fault," she explained, "Oh, Eli, sweetheart, why do you feel guilty about everything? Eli, change your clothes. I forgive you."
"Stop forgiving me. Stop understanding me."
"But I love you."
"That's something else."
"But, sweetie, you *don't* have to dress like that. You didn't do anything. You don't have to feel guilty because...."

Neither the Jews nor the Gentiles are prepared for Eli's identity. It must be madness, there can be no other explanation, and they respond to him in this manner. Attendants humor him, get him away from the baby ("Excuse me, rabbi, you're wanted in the temple"), play him for the madman he is not. Eli is cogent, clear, utterly calm and fully in control of himself. There is no chewing on slippers in closets (an activity associated with his earlier breakdowns), but the men in the white suits grab him and carry him off, tearing off his jacket and his sleeve. "Then a needle slid under his skin. The drug calmed his soul, but did not reach it down where the blackness had reached."

Roth has written a story dealing with the theme of denial. He has focused on the disappearance of Jewish heritage in a world of material plenty but spiritual poverty. He has done so, moreover, with the same direct pointedness which characterized the older, apparently dead literary traditions of Yiddish. The setting is familiar; once again we find ourselves in a family environment, dealing with a husband and wife. Above all, Roth specifically concentrates on a uniquely Jewish problem. Obviously, the same preoccupations of the old world *shtetl* have altered in the specifics. Even the interests of the immigrant generation of the American ghetto are not his primary concern. Roth has followed the Jew into his new prosperity, but he has followed him with the eye of the Yiddish writer filled with the experience of the Jewish dilemma, regardless of the location. In this case, Roth is not suggesting that the Jew is encountering the tyranny of the old world *shtetl*. Tevye's problems were different. With the Jews of Woodenton, Roth underlines the new tyranny for the Jew in America, one that he has created for himself by fleeing from his Jewish identity.

The Flight of Malamud's Shlemihls

Even earlier than Roth, Bernard Malamud's attention was drawn to the problem of Jewish identity in America, and particularly to the quest of the young American Jew to rid himself of the "problem" of his Jewishness. Like Roth, Malamud deals in characteristics which are familiar to the *shtetl* and at the same time obviously unique to the American scene. His ironic heroes are flawed young Americans, not quite able to fulfill their dreams or images of themselves; slightly short, slightly neurotic, they are unmistakably the new world *shlemihls* with certain characteristics of the Old-World *luftmensh*. In the American context this means that they do not wish to be Jews, but cannot become non-Jews, in spite of all their efforts to free themselves from the burden. They touch, like the old *luftmenshen,* neither heaven nor earth and remain suspended in midair.

Such an individual is Henry Levin, the central figure in Malamud's story "The Lady of the Lake." [11] Levin, a former floor walker at Macy's department store, has come into a small inheritance and has decided to travel in Europe. In Paris he signs the register "Henry R. Freeman," in a scarcely arcane effort to gain a new identity. What is it that Levin wants to be free of? "He did not look Jewish, could pass as not—had." As he looks in the mirror, contemplating a future free from his past, his hopes rest on meeting a strange, exotic European woman, sweeping her off her feet, and then escaping to San Francisco as Henry Freeman, Gentile, to a new life. On an exotic island in the north of Italy he has found a beautiful creature, the hope for his future life. But the woman he has selected ironically seems to have an obsession. She keeps asking Henry whether he is Jewish. Levin-Freeman, slightly paranoid, suspects that she has some reason for questioning him and without hesitation denies his Jewishness three times, without any pang of conscience. "What had it brought him but headaches, inferiorities, unhappy memories?" After the final denial she unhappily announces that she cannot marry him, "because I hoped you were." She raises her sleeve to reveal a tattoo received at Buchenwald, then announces to the astonished suitor that her family is Jewish, and her heritage means too much to her to marry a non-Jew. Finally, too late, Levin-Freeman sputters: "Listen I—I am—," but she disappears, along with his hope for happiness.

Malamud's self-hating, self-denying Jews are comical characters. They attempt to make up for their emotional and physical deficiencies by convincing themselves that they possess special qualities, qualities usually found in handsome, self-possessed, striking Gentile men. When Henry first sees his Italian beauty, his thoughts turn to his own physical image with total self-consciousness.

> He was aware of his background and certain other disadvantages: but he also knew he wasn't a bad-looking guy, even, it could be said, quite on the handsome side. Though a pin-prick bald at the back of his noggin—not more than a dime could adequately cover—his head of hair was alive, expressive. Freeman's gray eyes were clear, unenvious, nose well molded, the mouth generous. He has well-proportioned arms and legs and his stomach lay respectfully flat. He was a bit short, but on him, he knew, it barely showed. One of his former girl friends had told him she sometimes thought of him as tall. This counter-balanced the occasions when he had thought of himself as short.

It is Woody Allen wishing he were Robert Redford, but Malamud never ceases to remind his awkward hero that he cannot succeed. It is impossible to be debonair if one wears a bathing suit under one's slacks. Henry runs hopelessly after his Christian princess as he runs from his Jewish identity. He is prepared to live the lie of "passing." Malamud has created a *luftmensh* of the emotions, no longer an economic tragedy, but a past-denying young man for whom Buchenwald has no meaning. He dangles between two worlds, unable to find meaning in either. Malamud's point is clear, his picture of the postwar generation as sharp and as critical as is Roth's.

This was a type which occupied Malamud for a while. In "The Last Mohican" [12] it is Arthur Fidelman, and once again

Malamud uses, ironically, the flight *to* Europe *from* America as a mode of escape. Fidelman, from the first sentence, is the *luftmensh-shlemihl,* a self-confessed failure as a painter who has come to Italy to write the definitive study of Giotto. Malamud does not burden him with a new name to symbolize his effort at rejecting his past. Instead, Fidelman arrives carrying his first chapter in a pigskin briefcase. As if that were not enough, at the very moment of his arrival at the Rome railroad station, he is confronted by a figure from a different world, a skinny stranger with baggy pants and outstretched hand, a beggar whose first word to Fidelman is "Shalom"! Fidelman, who has travelled five thousand miles and is wearing a new mustache to alter his identity, is picked out of a crowd by a Jewish *shnorrer* who immediately asks for a loan.

Shimon Susskind is no ordinary beggar, for he, too, has roots which identify his species. He is clearly a postwar type, a refugee and survivor of the death camps. After leaving Europe, he traveled to Israel, but could not survive there. He tells the reluctant listener Fidelman that the climate was too harsh and the work too hard. So he is living illegally in Rome, dealing in all and sundry, and asking Jewish-looking foreigners if they speak Yiddish. The annoyed Fidelman asks him what he lives on, and Susskind answers: "I eat air." Malamud has created a latter-day Menachem Mendel, the impoverished but perpetually optimistic Jewish hustler struggling for a living in an alien world. In a sense, Menachem Mendel was "at home" in this world, because he knew that everyone he spoke to was at least Jewish, that Tevye would understand him and his efforts to survive would fit, even though tragically, into the world order. Susskind is a ghost from another world, a Displaced Person living on his wits, who still believes the whole world should be Jewish, and above all, that Jews should take care of one another.

In Fidelman, however, he meets a Jew who wants no part of him, and this he cannot understand. Fidelman runs and

Susskind chases, until one day Fidelman returns to his hotel room to discover that his most cherished possession, the pigskin briefcase with the chapter on Giotto, has been stolen. He immediately suspects the wandering Jew, and now the roles are reversed. The pursued becomes the pursuer. Fidelman's search for Susskind, however, becomes obviously more than just that. The days drag on into weeks and months, Fidelman loses the American tourist image and takes on the dark, haggard characteristics of the natives. His search takes him into the dank, airless streets of the Jewish quarter of Rome, the old ghetto. Here, Fidelman's inquiries turn into a symbolic quest for his own identity. Gradually he comes to understand the meaning of Susskind and all that he represents. He finally runs into the poor wretch selling holy beads in front of St. Peter's, and once again the beggar asks him for a loan to buy stock; pictures of the Holy Mother are selling well. Fidelman follows Susskind back into the labyrinths of the ghetto, to the squalid hovel he calls home; gradually, the briefcase and its contents lose all their former meaning, and an insight begins to come to Fidelman. Earlier, in a fit of anger when desperately trying to get rid of the pest, Fidelman had exploded: "Am I then responsible for you then, Susskind?" and the hustler had loudly replied: "Who else?" As he looks around him in the ghetto, at the centuries-old faces and buildings, Fidelman is filled with the same experience that Eli Peck had when he put on the black threads of the Hassid. He begins to *feel* the experience of Jewish identity.

Suddenly Susskind, who had denied all knowledge of the affair, thrusts the briefcase, now empty, into Fidelman's hands. At first furious, he curses the peddler, who flees for his life but yells back, "I did you a favor. The words were there, but the spirit was missing." Fidelman chases after him with murder in his eye, but just as suddenly, enlightenment comes to him: "... moved by all that he had lately learned, [he] had a triumphant insight. 'Susskind, come back!' he shouted, half sobbing. . . . All is forgiven.' " But the *luftmensh* is gone. "When last seen he was still running."

Malamud ends his story on the upbeat. His Jewish *shlemihl*, escaping from an unwanted past, rediscovered that past in the life of a miserable, haunting outcast lost in time. Fidelman's redemption comes about when he accepts his Jewishness, and Malamud reaffirms in this dubious hero the hopes for the future of the Jewish identity. As long as there are Susskinds to remind the Fidelmans, the Jew will survive.

Malamud prefers to have his stories and his heroes come to a modestly positive conclusion, and he particularly enjoys the formula of confrontation between the Jew in need of some outside intervention and an old *shtetl* type, a symbolic reminder of the continuity of Yiddishkeit and the Jewish experience.

In Leo Finkle, a young rabbinical student, Malamud has created in "The Magic Barrel" [13] still another dilemma for the Jew in America. Finkle is not one of Malamud's escapist *shlemihls*, but he is faced with an identity crisis as a Jew that is even more serious. Malamud, through Finkle, examines the decay of spiritual Judaism, the state of things in terms of the relationship of the individual to his God. Finkle is very much the rabbi in America, or at least the rabbinical student in America, no longer a starving scholar gathering crumbs from the *nogid's* table, but now a graduate of Yeshiva University in New York. He is looking through the advertisements of the *Jewish Daily Forward* for marriage brokers, because one of his classmates told him that it would be easier to get a congregation if he were married. So, quite pragmatically, Finkle contacts Pinye Salzman, one of a dying breed, the matchmaker in America.

He has all the characteristics of the type; in the Tevye stories he was called Ephraim, and he was the used-car salesman of the *shtetl*, willing and able to make a deal on any boy or girl, making the homely seem attractive, the old seem young. Salzman is skin and bones, a toothless wisp of a man with dirty index cards covered with information: "Lily H. High School teacher. Regular. Not a substitute. Has savings and new Dodge car. Lived in Paris one year. Father a successful dentist thirty-five years. Interested in a professional man. Well Americanized family. Wonderful opportunity.... Her age is thirty-two years." Again we are dealing with the *yichus* of the old world, now translated into American terms. Education is still of paramount importance, followed closely by *parnosseh* ("A Regular. No substitute.") When Salzman returns to inform Finkle that he had made an error in calculating the woman's age, that Lily H. was really only twenty-nine, Finkle decides to take a chance. During an arranged walk on Riverside Drive, he discovers the folly of his efforts. He meets instead of the Lily H. described by Salzman "a woman past thirty-five and aging rapidly." Worse yet, he realizes that Salzman has described him to the woman as a religious person with some special relationship to God, a *tzaddik,* called to his vocation by a unique talent for spiritual thought. Her enthusiastic questioning of him leads Finkle to admit to her and, finally, to himself, " 'I think,' he said in a strained manner, 'that I came to God not because I loved Him, but because I did not.' This confession he spoke harshly because its unexpectedness shook him."

Finkle, having faced for the first time in his life the spiritual vacuum of his religious conviction, despairs. He thinks of giving up his studies, quitting the Yeshiva, confessing his failure. He grows haggard, desolate. But like so many of Malamud's heroes, self-awareness and understanding come after the pain of reenactment, and gradually his despair turns into something like reconciliation with himself: "Out of this, however, he drew the consolation that he was a Jew, and that a Jew suffered. But, gradually, as the long and terrible week drew to a close, he regained his composure and some idea of purpose in life." Finkle has reached a new plateau, one more meaningful and genuine; he informs Salzman that he intends to marry for love, and not in order to get a congregation.

While rummaging through some photos which the marriage broker has inadvertently left behind, Finkle is suddenly struck by a girl's face, filled with love and at the same time with pain and despair. Once again, the roles are changed. Again, the prey becomes the hunter; Finkle, who had trouble keeping Salzman away from his door, now races up to the Bronx to find the matchmaker in order to identify the picture. In his description of Finkle's world, Malamud makes no effort at hiding the roots of the matchmaker. Finkle asks Salzman's wife for the location of the matchmaker's office, and she replies, "In the air ... In his socks." Finkle, depressed, begs Mrs. Salzman to tell her husband that he is urgently wanted, and then returns home to his meager Manhattan room. To his astonishment, Salzman is already waiting for him. When he asks, "How did you get here before me?" Salzman, out of breath, but still the *luftmensh* to the end, almost carried by the wind, gasps, "I rushed!" When Finkle shows Salzman the picture, the matchmaker is horrified to see that it is his daughter Stella, apparently a fallen girl whom Salzman describes as a wild animal (in Yiddish the phrase *vilde Chaya*). Her photo did not belong among Salzman's customers. But Finkle has now become a tower of emotional persistence. He sees his entire life's meaning tied to the fate of this strange young woman, and he brings to his meeting with her a new energy and purpose. When he meets Stella, finally, standing under a lamp post smoking a cigarette, he races toward her, flowers in his hand, a new life before him, one with meaning.

Malamud wants to demonstrate how a life without purpose, the aimless and undirected existence of an isolated Jew in America, can be given purpose. It only happens when others are involved, and, in this case, a couple of *shlemihl-luftmenshen* share their unhappiness and benefit from this experience. Finkle will find his hoped-for redemption in the arms of the wayward Stella. His rabbinical commitment which, until the meeting with Salzman and his daughter, lacked any relationship to a divine calling, suddenly takes on the spark of holiness, the sense of mission and calling we encountered in the *tzaddikim* of the *shtetl*.

Finkle serves as a bridge between the New-World young Jews of Malamud's fiction, those who are in flight from Jewishness, and another of his favorite character types, the old Jew, lonely and wretched, isolated and unable to find in America any sense of community or family to see him through his old age. These older *shlemihls* have lost the touch of humanity, of faith, which marked a Tevye. They live cut off from the nourishment of the *shtetl* which even at its most wretched provided Jews with a sense of belonging. Malamud's old Jews do not even belong, they cannot communicate with anyone and seem to be consumed by the grayness of the desperate environment in which Malamud places them. Yet Malamud is determined to redeem them, to save them, either by a reaffirmation of their traditional faith or through an experience with another human being. In his novel *The Assistant*,[14] set in the American environment, and in his *shtetl* world recasting of the Mendel Beiliss case, *The Fixer*,[15] Malamud forces redemption on his reluctant Jews.[16]

The Crisis of Generations
What uniquely characterizes almost all of the writers we might identify as Jewish-American, and clearly connects the three under consideration here, is the attention paid to the trauma of family disintegration, conflict, and alienation, particularly within the frame of reference of old-world traditions and new-world values. These values are not all identified with the green sterility of suburbia. Malamud is much more comfortable in the narrow streets of the American ghetto, in transitional neighborhoods turning from Jewish to black. His

old Jews are generally men who seem to have been left behind. They live in dark tenements, or in the back of failing
candy stores and groceries, waiting for the end. Saul Bellow
selects as the site for his confrontation of the American Jew
in crisis the big city, to him a symbol of all that is alienating,
cold, and detached, the very opposite of the *shtetl*, where it
was considered an insult to mind one's own business. Philip
Roth's unique versatility permits him to work successfully in
both of these environments as well as in suburbia. *Portnoy's
Complaint* is very much the big city novel, his story "Epstein" much closer to Malamud in flavor and tone, while
"Goodbye, Columbus" and "Eli the Fanatic" take us beyond
the city limits.

In each author, the primary concern is family, and they
share a common orientation: that American life and its associated freedom can undermine essential familial bonds. Malamud remains the least complicated. The nature of his family
crises is quite similar to those encountered in the Tevye
stories; in fact, it is the crisis of father and daughter, most
frequently. In "The First Seven Years" [17] the shoemaker Feld
wants nothing more for his daughter Miriam than a better
life than he had in his miserable *shtetl* in Europe. He dreams
of a doctor, a lawyer, some professional man, and when he
spots a young student customer, he sets himself to arranging
a meeting. But Max is a materialist, somewhat vulgar, utterly
unimaginative, a student of accountancy. To Feld, he is a potential C.P.A. son-in-law; to Miriam he is a bore. Feld is completely oblivious to what the reader sees in the relationship
between Miriam and Feld's morose assistant, a refugee
named Sobel, a silent and mysterious survivor of the death
camps. He gives her books, shares his deep, personal tragedy
with her. Sobel quits in fury when he sees Feld's intentions
concerning the student. Ironically, without the reliable assistant who really runs the business for the sick proprietor, Feld
cannot survive. He suffers a heart attack, Miriam disappoints

him by rejecting the young man he has selected for her, and out of desperation he has to seek out the wayward assistant and beg him to return. In the grimness of the dark room in a boarding house, Feld asks Sobel to return, and the DP, filled with fury, explodes, denouncing Feld for ignoring his overtures to Miriam. In Feld's eyes, a life for Miriam with Sobel would be one filled with misery; he wants more, seeks a better life for his daughter, one, like Tevye's dream, filled with material blessings. Miriam, however, searches for a spiritual satisfaction which she can find only with the ugly cobbler twice her age but who, in the concentration camps, has experienced something which has meaning for both of them. Feld, with a sigh of relief, reluctantly comes to some insight into the meaning of Sobel's experience, into the abyss which had almost destroyed this survivor of the death camps. Miriam and Sobel share this, and Feld finally permits Sobel to return to the store as a potential suitor for his daughter. When he leaves Sobel, Feld walks through the night air with a stronger step and firmer resolve. The pain in his chest is gone.

Malamud prefers to take this potential family tragedy and to turn it into a modest triumph of reaffirmation of Jewish identity. Like all these American-Jewish writers, he confronts in almost all of his writings the moral question of identity, although he is more restrained than either Roth or Bellow. His family crises seem to have a way of working out; the old Jews—Manishevitz the tailor in "The Angel Levine," Kessler the egg candler and Gruber the landlord in "The Mourners," Lieb the baker in "The Loan"—start out as isolated figures, cut off from any Jewish moral experience, and then Malamud forces them to confront an issue which makes for a critical understanding of their lives. Inevitably, they hit the bottom, but then, by an affirmation of faith in someone, rise on a spiritual and moral wave which leaves them strengthened physically as well as metaphysically.

Roth and Bellow are less sanguine. Their reaction to the crisis of family is highly critical and aggressive. In their examination of Jewish social life in America, their attitude is one of unabashed outrage and anger. Roth's stories "Goodbye, Columbus" and "Epstein" are acute examples of his sharp observation of and commitment to the problem of estrangement.

In "Goodbye, Columbus," Roth offers a variety of subjects for moral scrutiny, but it is the alienation between parent and child which he describes as the most serious of the aberrations in modern American life. In most other respects, Roth's barbs are no different from those of a Sinclair Lewis, except that the Babbitts of this story are *nouveau riche* Jews who have moved out of the Newark ghetto, into the upper middle-class country club setting of Short Hills, New Jersey. Roth takes this opportunity to score the quality of American Jewish life, just as he had in "Eli the Fanatic," but with more variety. He berates Jews for lack of social consciousness, particularly lack of sensitivity toward racism and prejudice. He paints a picture of a decaying Newark, with Jews fleeing to the suburbs, leaving the dilapidated tenements to the blacks, victims of prejudice from Jews and Gentiles alike. But, says Roth's spokesman, Neil Klugman, the Jews should know better, because they've been through it. Klugman (Roth, Malamud, and Bellow repeatedly use Yiddishisms to give added symbolic meaning to the names of their characters) is a remnant of the ghetto whose parents have moved to Arizona for reasons of health. He lives with an over-protective aunt, a Malamudian character, in Newark's inner city, but he yearns for the good life of the suburbs, embodied in the style of the Patimkin family (distant friends of friends) whom Neil approaches through their daughter Brenda during a summer vacation from college. Roth takes a broad swipe at the non-intellectual life of American college students, whose main activity seems to be reliving sports fantasies and joining fraternities. His picture of the mindless noninvolvement and insipid occupations of this generation of the '50s is as mordant as any found in contemporary American literature. Brenda and her fellow students from the Ivy League and Big Ten Midwestern universities create an image of dull socializing, vulgar materialism, and complete unawareness of the larger world around them.

He reserves his narrower focus and sharpest picture for the individual members of the Patimkin family. The father is an amiable, good-hearted man, the proud owner of Patimkin Kitchen and Bathroom Sinks, energetic, determined to give his children everything, a successful businessman who made his modest fortune during the war, selling his goods to the army. He is a *nogid* with neither vices nor virtues; if there is a positive side to the character, it rests in his basic human instincts. However, as a parent he has produced two children of no particular distinction. Ron Patimkin is a graduate of Ohio State University, a college athlete with all the traits implied by the mindless world of the American "jock." He plans to gravitate quite naturally into his father's business. His fiancée, Harriet Ehrlich, is a smiling, nodding creature, the perfect daughter-in-law, who will allow her prospective family to pick out the furniture, the apartment, the neighborhood, indeed, the number of children they will have. The real conflict, the deeper, troubling aspect of this family which Roth concentrates on is the relationship between Mrs. Patimkin and her daughter Brenda. Mrs. Patimkin emerges as a mindless product of Jewish consciousness in America. She is not a suburbanite of the Woodenton, Long Island, mold. She is Jewish to the core, a member of Hadassah, a socially active club woman, but, like her female counterparts in the *shtetl,* actually ignorant of any knowledge of Judaism in its religious or secular heritage. She is simply Jewish, and that is all she requires of anyone. Yet she has entered into a love-hate relationship with her daughter who, because of her youth, challenges Mrs. Patimkin's "right" to remain young and attractive. The single most important aspect of her life is her unchallenged position as dominant female in the family. She cannot tolerate the presence of Brenda, seeks out a vapid bride for her son, dominates her husband and attempts to drive a wedge between him and his daughter. Brenda is confused and unable to cope with her mother's aggressive behavior.

From Roth's perspective, he looks down on the life of the well-off Jews in America and expresses his disgust at the price of prosperity. He observes a Jewishness devoid of any expression not merely of faith (one need not be an observant or even believing Jew, in Roth's mind) but of any of the great tradition of learning, humanity, or concern with the essential qualities of the Jewish past. Above all, he observes the state of the Jewish family and sees a conflict between generations which is abnormal and destructive.

In "Goodbye, Columbus," Roth indicts the parents. In "Epstein" he is just as hard on the youth. The Patimkin children lack the essential qualities of mind because they have been brought up in a world which paid no attention to these qualities. In "Epstein" we see the social conscience of the young developing in a manner as unattractive as the materialism of the older generation. Again, the Jewish family in America appears to be in a state of decay, preoccupied with problems of alienation. Lou Epstein is a small businessman driven to despair by isolation. His life had been tragic since the death of his only son Herbie at age eleven from polio.[18] His daughter Sheila is a misdirected radical who has taken up with a hippie folk singer, and both are filled with contempt for the world of Epstein. The reader, however, feels a deep and tragic compassion for Lou, as he contemplates his daughter's life and wonders where he and his wife Goldie went wrong:

> What happened to that little pink-skinned baby? What year, what month did those skinny ankles grow thick as logs, the peaches-and-cream turn to pimples? That lovely

child was now a twenty-three-year-old woman with "a social conscience"! Some conscience, he thought. She hunts
all day for a picket line to march in so at night she can
come home and eat like a horse. . . .

This is more than just Epstein talking, it is also Roth. The
story is filled with scorn for the Jewish youth dogmati-
cally and contemptuously rejecting the world of their parents,
completely lacking any understanding of the struggles and
pains of bringing up children. Lou Epstein is finally driven,
out of despair, into an almost comical adulterous relationship
with an elderly neighbor; he develops a rash and his daughter accuses him of contracting syphilis. Only a near-fatal
heart attack, aided by the attending physician's assurance
that the rash will clear up completely, brings a reconciliation
with his wife. As in his other stories which deal with the
conflicts of the American Jew, Roth creates a world devoid
of those traditional supports encountered in the *shtetl*. The
world of the Epsteins and the Patimkins, of the Jews of
Woodenton, is one taken up entirely by the economics of
making it in America, and of demonstrating that you have
achieved something to those around you. The price for Lou
Epstein was great. He no longer talks to his brother Sol and
hasn't seen him for years—they fought over the business.
Mr. Patimkin and the businessmen of Woodenton have no
time for anything else. Eli Peck begins to understand what is
missing, and he is taken for a madman. The state of the Jewish family in Roth's picture is grim, and it has been perceived
as such by those people who constitute his reading public.
Many join him in crying out; others are embarrassed by him
and consider Roth's outspoken criticism an outrage with distinctly anti-Semitic implications. *Goodbye, Columbus,* the
collection of stories which appeared in 1960, was awarded
the Daroff Memorial Award of the Jewish Book Council of
America. But there was such an enormous outburst of criticism at this that the Council had to offer a disclaimer and

stated that henceforth the award would be given to works "characterized by an affirmative expression of Jewish values." Ironically, Roth's vision of the society he writes about is more in the Yiddish tradition of social criticism than perhaps any other writer we identify as being in the Jewish-American tradition. Roth is crying out against the disintegration of kinship values which have been the essence of Jewish survival through the centuries. He portrays this world as decadent because through satire, he hopes, will come realization.

Roth wants to hope. Like Malamud, he has a guarded, optimistic dream for the future regeneration of the Jewish family in America. Saul Bellow's despair, however, is total, his rage consuming, but like the others, he implores the Jew in America to rediscover his roots if he has any hopes at all of surviving. It is in his novel, *Mr. Sammler's Planet*,[18] that Bellow articulates the full expression of his distress concerning the state of Jewish consciousness in America. Once again, the author's particular concern is a generational one, but the special anger is reserved for the Jewish youth of the '60s.

Bellow must be considered America's premier serious writer, and since the early 1940s he has produced a body of writing unequaled in quality by any other writer of American fiction. From the beginning there has, furthermore, always been at least the suggestion of his Jewish roots. His first major work, *Dangling Man,* has more than just the titular relationship to the idea of the *luftmensh.* From that point on, his central characters have usually been young Jewish males in search of a personal identity. Bellow, like Malamud (*The Natural*[19]) and Roth (*When She Was Good*[20]), has also attempted a completely "Gentile" novel (*Henderson the Rain King*[21]). But, inevitably, he has returned to the analysis of *shlemihl*-like types in search of meaning.

The experience of the '60s helped to re-focus Bellow's vision. Until then, he represented a distinctly liberal-Jewish intellectual tradition which saw him consistently aligned with the causes of civil rights, dissent, and generally avant-garde ideas. The student unrest, the violence on the college campuses, his perception that America, with its soft intellectualism and over-committed liberal enlightenment, was growing decadent, and that Jewish-American youth represented, more than any other group, this spirit of decay, created for Bellow the atmosphere which produced his jeremiad, *Mr. Sammler's Planet.*

Bellow, in the strongest terms he knows, reasserts the traditions of Jewish roots, of *mishpoche,* of family, in the face of a generation of young people who have forgotten what and who they are. Instead of his typical young hero, Bellow places the seventy-year-old Mr. Sammler at the center of the narrative. Sammler himself had been a Jew running from his heritage. As a member of the cultivated British Bloomsbury group, he preferred upper-crust London society and assimilation. When circumstances brought him back to his native Poland in 1939, he rediscovered his Jewishness in the Nazi concentration camps where he finally arrived. He saw his wife shot and thrown into a pit with hundreds of other bodies. By a miracle, Sammler survived certain death in the same forest grave, found his way to the Partisans, and learned to kill in order to live. All the sensitive and elegant civilization of England in the '30s, the genteel anti-semitism which Sammler himself had indulged in, all of this paled against the realities of survival in the Polish forests. After the war, Sammler and his half-mad daughter were rescued by an American relative, Dr. Arnold Gruner, who constantly searched through the displaced persons list for relatives.

Growing old in America, Sammler contemplates his life and his Jewishness. More than anything else, he tries to understand what has happened to a generation of young people seemingly corrupted by permissiveness, unrestrained sexuality, overcommitted democracy, and an overwhelming need for instant gratification. The only decent idea in the world of

Mr. Sammler seems to be Arnold Gruner's sense of the past, of the Jewish heritage, of the world of his fathers. But, Gruner is dying, Sammler is attacked by a black pickpocket in his own apartment house, he is mocked and ridiculed by arrogant student revolutionaries, and beyond that, he witnesses the decay and breakdown of civilization, symbolized by the special horror of the jungle which New York City has become.[23] Above all, there is the youth, especially the Jewish youth. Tragically, both Gruner and Sammler have failed as parents. Gruner's two children, Wallace and Angela, have enjoyed all the material benefits and have experienced none of the spiritual ones. She is a nymphomaniac, a jet-setting swinger who throws parties for "defense funds for black murderers and rapists." Wallace, an almost-Ph.D. in several subjects, cannot hold on to anything. They are both neurotic, deep into analysis and dependent on psychiatrists, *luftmenshen* to the core. Sammler's daughter is a parody of shallow intellectuals and middle-aged eccentrics, into causes which they do not understand and ideas which are beyond their comprehension. She is also a victim of the Holocaust, as are several other misfits in Sammler's circle. Sammler looks around him and sees himself as a "collector," a *sammler* in Yiddish, of wretched Jewish types. He and Gruner enjoy talking about the old days, and they share an enthusiasm for the State of Israel. These two refugees from the Jewish world of the past represent all that remains of continuity with that world. Their experience is emotional, instinctive, deeply personal. Sammler no longer trusts the petty intellectuals, the liberal, modern assimilationists. Yet he is helpless to do anything but lament, and to contemplate what may be the final phase in the history of the wandering Jew, as he thinks of abandoning the earth in favor of, perhaps, the moon.

Sammler stands alone, more alone than Tevye ever was. For Tevye's children represented at least a world still in motion, one which Jewish children might alter while not completely abandoning it. In Sammler's solitary end, the continuity of the past has been completely broken. Bellow, through old Sammler, seems to be saying that the Jew has come to the end of the line in America.

Bellow snapped out of this grim mood soon after the excesses of the '60s had faded into memory. Still, he articulates very well the growing concern of the older generation of American Jews with their past, with their roots. That world, however, is gone. One must look for another "connection," another experience of Jewish continuity. Sammler had expressed it with his sense of identity with the State of Israel. Bellow, too, now himself in his sixties, more than ever falls back on his Jewish past. The anger with the younger generation seems to have abated. For a moment, though, in *Mr. Sammler's Planet,* this American author found himself thoroughly involved in the traditions of *Yiddishkeit* and the preoccupation with the disintegration of the Jewish family.

Epilogue

From the very moralistic beginnings of Yiddish literature to the furious diatribes of Roth and Bellow, Jewish writers, whether in the Pale or in America, continued to ask the same question: what will it take for the Jew to survive? There were two different replies. In the old world, the Yiddish writer first posed the problem, then answered by informing the Jewish audience that change was coming, that the old ways would be difficult to hold on to, and that somehow, the *shtetl* Jew must prepare himself and his family for the inevitable confrontation with the modern world.

The American-Jewish writers had the opportunity to study the effects of this confrontation, to observe how the old-world Jews had come to America and how they had been adopted by the land of opportunity. They noted the impact of freedom, of opportunity, and not quite a century after the beginning of that earlier confrontation, these writers began asking: What happened? How could a people, in such a brief period of time, so completely disengage themselves from traditions and ideals which had been ingrained in them for centuries, and which had survived travails of all kinds, slaughters, forced baptisms, even opportunities to assimilate?

There is a connection between the death of Tevye's wife Golde and old Sammler's benefactor Gruner. They have left behind children who have broken the chain of tradition forged over centuries. In Sholom Aleichem's world, the author is suggesting that out of the denial of traditional Judaism there might emerge a stronger breed, better able to cope with the uncertainties of the modern world. In Sholom Aleichem's world, the central characters could not deny their past. In the world of Malamud, Roth, and Bellow, the dubious heroes could not come to acknowledge their past.

In each case, the threat to the Jewish world is just as serious. The question of Jewish survival is one which all of these writers see as the pivotal one in their fictive world, and the battleground on which the struggle is fought is one on which the generations of Jewish families meet. Inevitably, this becomes the identification mark of something we might call "Jewish literature," regardless of the language in which it is written. Whether in Kafka's German or Schwarz-Bart's French, it is the conflict of generations which is the serious stuff of literature for the Jew, or, more specifically, the rights of the *father*. Kafka is perhaps the most Jewish of all writers in this respect! This strongly patriarchal orientation joins all of these writers who in one way or another struggle with the idea of survival.

The only certain victim of the trauma of confrontation has been the Yiddish language. It appears to be only a question of a few more generations before it goes the way of Latin and becomes a subject of historical interest, no longer a living tongue spoken by natives. Modernity, the spirit of change, the continued wanderings of the Jew have produced this fact, which some acknowledge sadly, others in a spirit of optimism. For the Jew has found another means of expression in Israel, and modern Hebrew has been reborn, to produce still another great literature, one which undoubtedly will once more demonstrate the Jewish preoccupation with *mishpoche*. Tevye's world is gone. We are not certain what will happen to Mr. Sammler's world. But if the Jew in America continues to show concern for the existence of a Jewish tradition in this country, it will be through the theme of family conflict that this concern will be expressed. For the Jew, survival of family means survival of the Jewish tradition.

A Selective Reference
Bibliography in English

There is a great deal of highly specialized literature available to the student interested in the various aspects of *Judaica*. The present study touches on the fields of literature, religion, sociology, psychology, history, and ethics, each of which sustains an enormous amount of writing in Yiddish, Hebrew, German, French, as well as English. The following bibliographical material is intended to serve the general English-speaking reader who might be interested in developing a background in these particular fields of Jewish Studies, yet who might not have access to the more esoteric materials in the subject.

Introduction: General Background

For general information, the *Encyclopedia Judaica* (Jerusalem: Keter Publishing House, 1971), is indisputably the best reference set available. Its nineteen volumes contain elegant articles on every conceivable subject written by the best Jewish scholars in the world. For home use, there is the one-volume *Encyclopedia of the Jewish Religion,* edited by Werblowsky and Wigoder (New York: Holt, Rinehart & Winston, 1966), which deals with subjects not just religious in nature. The following is a brief list of useful general books touching all aspects of Jewish history:

Agus, J. B., *The Meaning of Jewish History* (New York: Abelard-Schuman, 1963).

Ausubel, Nathan, *A Pictorial History of the Jewish People* (New York: Crown Publishers, 1953).

Baron, Salo W., *A Social and Religious History of the Jews* (New York: Columbia University Press, 1937, revised and enlarged to eight volumes, 1952).

Bamberger, B. J., *The Story of Judaism* (New York: The Union of American Hebrew Congregations, 1957).

Dimont, Max I., *Jews, God and History* (New York: Simon and Schuster, 1962). Popular Jewish history, at times too imaginative.

Dubnow, S. M., *An Outline of Jewish History* (New York: Max Maisel, 1925). Three volumes translated from the Russian.

Finkelstein, Louis, editor, *The Jews: Their History, Culture, and Religion*, two volumes (New York: Harper & Brothers, 1949; 3rd edition, Philadelphia: Jewish Publication Society of America); later revised and in paperback (New York: Schocken Books, 1971). Excellent collection of essays.

Graetz, Heinrich, *History of the Jews* (Philadelphia: The Jewish Publication Society, 1891). A six-volume history which is itself a remarkable historical document of 19th century views.

Martin, Bernard, and Silver, Daniel Jeremy, *A History of Judaism*, Vol. I, *Abraham to Maimonides;* Vol. II, *Europe and the New World* (New York: Basic Books, 1974). The most useful and readable accounts available in paperback.

Roth, Cecil, *A Short History of the Jewish People,* 2nd edition revised (London: East and West Library, 1969).

————, *A History of the Jews: From the Earliest Times to the Six Day War,* revised edition (New York: Schocken Books, 1974).

Sachar, Abram L., *A History of the Jews,* third edition (New York: Alfred A. Knopf, 1948).

Chapter 1: The Roots and Growth of Yiddish

Since Yiddish is basically a Germanic language, in almost every general history of Germanic linguistics one encounters routine discussions of the linguistic evolution of Yiddish from Middle High German. There is also a great deal of material written in German on the development of Yiddish, and for any serious scholar or for the student interested in going beyond a superficial understanding of Yiddish, a knowledge of German is essential. Furthermore, there is considerable activity concerning the historical origins of Yiddish at the Yiddish Institute for Research (YIVO) in New York City and the Weinreich Center for Yiddish Studies at Columbia University. Similarly, non-Yiddish-speaking Jewish linguistic studies focusing on Sephardic Jews, German Jews, and Yiddish in America, continue to appear.

The other significant aspects of this chapter concentrate on the relationship between Jew and Arab during the Golden Age of the Caliphates; the figure of Maimonides; Rashi and the French-Jewish community; the earliest forms of Yiddish literature and the beginnings of German Jewry.

Arab and Jew

Ben-Sasson, H. H. and Ettinger, S., eds., *Jewish Society Through the Ages*, paperback (New York: Schocken Books, 1971), contains an essay by S. D. Goitein, "Jewish Society and Institutions under Islam," pp. 170–184.

Fischel, W. J., *The Jews in the Economic and Political Life of Medieval Islam* (London: Royal Asiatic Society, 1937).

Goitein, S. D., *Jews and Arabs: Their Contacts Through the Ages* (New York: Schocken Books, 1955). Probably the best book on the subject.

Katsh, A. I., *Judaism in Islam* (New York: New York University Press, 1954). Concentrates on religious integration of the two faiths.

Mann, J., *The Jews in Egypt and Palestine Under the Fatamid Caliphs* (London: Oxford University Press, 1920–1922).

Neuman, A. A., *The Jews in Spain* (Philadelphia: Jewish Publication Society of America, 1948).

Maimonides

Bratton, F. G., *Maimonides, Medieval Modernist* (Boston: Beacon Press, 1967).

Friedlander, M., tr., *Guide to the Perplexed*, by Maimonides, with introduction (London: Routledge and Co., 1910).

Goitein, S. D., *A Mediterranean Society*, 3 volumes (Berkeley: University of California Press, 1967–71). A three-volume study of the entire Egyptian and Spanish societies out of which Maimonidean philosophy and medicine grew.

Twersky, Isadore, editor, *A Maimonides Reader* (New York: Behrman House, 1972). The best selection and an excellent introduction.

Spaniard and Jew

Baer, Y. F., *The History of the Jews in Christian Spain* (Philadelphia: Jewish Publication Society of America, 1961). The two-volume definitive study.

Neuman, A., *The Jews in Spain*, op. cit.

Husik, Isaac, *A History of Medieval Jewish Philosophy*, paperback (New York: Atheneum, 1969).

Roth, Cecil, *A History of the Marranos* (Philadelphia: Jewish Publication Society of America, 1932).

Rashi and the Early Franco-German Judaism

Ben-Sasson, H. H., "The Northern European Jewish Community and Its Ideals," in *Jewish Society Through the Ages,* Ben-Sasson and Ettinger, eds. (New York: Schocken Books, 1972).

Blumenfield, S. M., *Master of Troyes: A Study of Rashi the Educator* (New York: Behrman House, 1946).

Hailperin, H., *Rashi and the Christian Scholars* (Pittsburgh: University of Pittsburgh Press, 1963).

Kisch, G., *The Jews of Medieval Germany* (Chicago: University of Chicago Press, 1948).

Liber, M, *Rashi* (Philadelphia: Jewish Publication Society of America, 1906).

Lowenthal, M., *The Jews of Germany* (Philadelphia: Jewish Publication Society of America, 1936).

Rabinowitz, L. I., *The Social Life of the Jews of Northern France in the XII–XIV Centuries as Reflected in the Rabbinical Literature of the Period* (London: Edward Goldston, 1936).

Twersky, Isadore, "Aspects of the Social and Cultural History of Provencal Jewry," in *Jewish Society Through the Ages,* op. cit.

The Yiddish Language

The best and most thoroughly comprehensive essay is contained in the *Encyclopedia Judaica.* At this time there is no definitive study in English of the history and sources of the Yiddish language. The only such work, scholarly and scientific, is Salcia Landmann's study in German, *Jiddisch: Abenteuer einer Sprache* (Munich, Deutscher Taschenbuchverlag, 1964). The following are useful sources which deal partially with the early evolution of the Yiddish language.

Fishman, Joshua A., *Yiddish in America: Socio-linguistic Description and Analysis* (Bloomington: Indiana University Press, 1965).

Herzog, Marvin I., *The Yiddish Language of Northern Poland: Geography and History* (Bloomington: Indiana University Press, 1965).

——, ed., and others, *The Field of Yiddish: Studies in Language, Folklore, and Literature* (New York: Columbia University Press, 1969).

Samuel, Maurice, *In Praise of Yiddish* (New York: Cowles Book Company, 1971).

Weinreich, Uriel, ed., *The Field of Yiddish: Studies in Language, Folklore, and Literature,* two vols. (The Hague: Martinus Niejhoff, 1954 and 1965).

———, *College Yiddish* (New York: Columbia University Press, 1949). Still, in spite of its age, the only reliable college Yiddish grammar.

———, ed., *Modern Yiddish-English, English-Yiddish Dictionary* (New York: McGraw-Hill, 1968). A major lexicographical advancement over all previous Yiddish dictionaries.

Chapter 2: The Revolutions of Heart and Mind: Hassidism and Haskalah

Late Middle Ages, Renaissance, and Reformation

Abrahams, Israel, *Jewish Life in the Middle Ages* (Philadelphia: Jewish Publication Society of America, 1920).

Finkelstein, Louis, *Jewish Self-Government in the Middle Ages* (New York: Jewish Theological Seminary of America, 1924).

Katz, Jacob, *Exclusiveness and Tolerance: Jewish-Gentile Relations in Medieval and Modern Times* (London: Oxford University Press, 1961).

Landau, S. J., *Christian-Jewish Relations: A New Era in Germany as a Result of the First Crusade* (New York: Pageant Press, 1960).

Parkes, James, *The Conflict of the Church and the Synagogue: A Study in the Origins of Antisemitism,* Temple edition (New York: Atheneum, 1969).

Roth, Cecil, *History of the Jews of Italy* (Philadelphia: Jewish Publication Society of America, 1946).

———, *The Jews of the Renaissance* (Philadelphia: Jewish Publication Society of America, 1959).

———, *History of the Jews of Venice* (Philadelphia: Jewish Publication Society of America, 1930).

Runciman, Samuel, *A History of the Crusades,* three vols. (Cambridge: Cambridge University Press, 1951–1954).

Shohet, D. M., *The Court Jew in the Middle Ages* (New York: Commanday-Roth Co., 1931).

Zinberg, Issaac, *French and German Jewry in the Middle Ages,* Benjamin Martin, tr. (Cleveland: Case-Western Reserve University Press, 1972).

Luther

Ben-Sasson, H. H., "The Reformation in Contemporary Jewish Eyes," *Proceedings of the Israel Academy of Sciences and Humanities*, 1970.

———, "Jewish-Christian Disputation in the Setting of Humanism and Reformation in the German Empire," *Harvard Theological Review*, 1966.

Newman, L. I., *Jewish Influence on Christian Reform Movements* (New York: Columbia University Press, 1925).

Age of the False Messiahs and Emergence of Kabbalah

Gershom Scholem is the leading authority on the subject of Jewish mysticism and Kabbalistic literature.

Abelson, Jacob, *Jewish Mysticism* (London: Bell & Sons, 1913).

Blau, J. L., *The Christian Interpretation of the Cabala in the Renaissance* (New York: Columbia University Press, 1944).

Ginzberg, Louis, *The Cabala in Jewish Law and Lore* (Philadelphia: Jewish Publication Society of America, 1955).

Scholem, Gershom, *Major Trends in Jewish Mysticism*, revised for Schocken edition (New York: Schocken Books, 1946).

———, *On the Kabbalah and Its Symbolism* (New York: Schocken Books, 1965).

———, *The Messianic Idea in Judaism and Other Essays* (New York: Schocken Books, 1971). Covers all the false Messiahs of the period.

———, Sabbatai Sevi, *The Mystical Messiah* (Princeton: Princeton University Press, 1973). An exhaustive and remarkable study.

Sperling, Simon, and Levertoff, trs., *The Zohar* (London: Soncino Press, 1931–1934).

Trachtenberg, Joshua, *Jewish Magic and Superstition: A Study in Folk Religion*, Temple edition (New York: Atheneum, 1970).

Weiner, H., *Nine and One Half Mystics: The Kabbalah Today* (New York: Holt, Rinehart & Winston, 1969).

Hassidism

Martin Buber has been the great popularizer and exponent of Hassidism, and all of his major writings on the subject have been translated from the original German.

Ben-Amos and Mintz, trs., *In Praise of the Baal Shem Tov* (Bloomington: Indiana University Press, 1970). A collection of legends and tales concerning the founder of Hassidism, gathered by his followers.

A Selective Reference Bibliography in English

Buber, Martin, *Hasidism*, Greta Hort, tr. (New York: Philosophical Library, 1948).

——, *Hasidism and Modern Man*, Maurice Friedman, tr. (New York: Horizon Press, 1958).

——, *The Origin and Meaning of Hasidism*, Maurice Friedman, tr. (New York: Horizon Press, 1960).

——, *Tales of the Hasidim*, two vols., Olga Marx, tr. (New York: Schocken Books, 1947–1948).

——, *Tales of Rabbi Nahman*, Maurice Friedman, tr. (New York: Horizon Press, 1956).

Chavel, B., "Schneour Zalman of Liady," in L. Jung, ed., *Jewish Leaders* (New York: Bloch Publishing Company, 1953). An interesting study of the founder of the Lubavitcher Hassidim.

Dresner, S. H., *The Zaddik* (New York: Abelard-Schuman, 1960). A full-length study of the role of the rabbi in Hassidism.

Gersh, H. and Miller, "Satmar in Brooklyn," *Commentary*, vol. 28, 1959. An article dealing with the current orthodox Hassidim living in the Williamsburg section of Brooklyn. Somewhat more controversial, on the same subject, is Solomon Poll's *The Hasidic Community of Williamsburg* (New York: Schocken Books, 1969).

Ginzberg, Louis, *Students, Scholars, and Saints*, "The Gaon: Rabbi Elijah Wilna" (Philadelphia: Jewish Publication Society of America, 1928). An excellent description of the leading orthodox opponent to Hasidism at the time of its rise.

Minkin, J. S., *The Romance of Hasidism* (New York: Macmillan, 1955). This up-to-date second edition is an excellent companion.

Newman, L. I., *A Hasidic Anthology* (New York: Charles Scribner's Sons, 1934). Along with Buber's collections, excellent source of Hassidic materials.

Rabinowicz, H. M., *The World of Hasidism* (London: Vallentine, Mitchell, 1970).

Schneerson, Joseph, *Some Aspects of Chabad Chassidism* (Brooklyn: Kehot, 1957). An expression of the ideas of Lubavitcher Hassidism by the current hereditary leader of the movement.

Waxman and Noveck, editors, *Great Jewish Personalities in Ancient and Medieval Times*, "Vilna Gaon" (Washington, D.C.: B'nai Brith Department of Adult Education, 1959). Places the struggle between orthodoxy and Hassidism in an interesting light. Vilna as a seat of the enlightened orthodox opposing the emotion of Hassidism.

Weiner, H., "The Lubavitcher Movement," *Commentary,* vol. 23, 1957. An up-to-date account of the origins and developments of "liberal" Hassidism.

Mendelssohn and the Haskalah

Altman, Alexander, ed., *Studies in Nineteenth-Century Jewish Intellectual History* (Cambridge, MA: Harvard University Press, 1964).

———, *Moses Mendelssohn: A Biographical Study* (University: University of Alabama Press, 1973). The most reliable biography of Mendelssohn yet written.

Baron, S. W., "The Modern Age," in Schwarz, ed., *Great Ages and Ideas of the Jewish People* (New York: Random House, 1956).

Blau, J. L., *Modern Varieties of Judaism* (New York: Columbia University Press, 1966).

Hertzberg, Arthur, *The French Enlightenment and the Jews* (New York: Columbia University Press, 1968).

Mendelssohn, Moses, *Jerusalem,* Jospe, tr. (New York: Schocken Books, 1969).

Meyer, M. A., *The Origins of the Modern Jew* (Detroit: Wayne State University Press, 1967).

Petuchowski, J. J., *Prayer Book Reform in Europe* (New York: World Union for Progressive Judaism, 1968).

Philipson, David, *The Reform Movement in Judaism,* revised edition (New York: KTAV, 1967).

Raisin, J. S., *The Haskalah Movement in Russia* (Philadelphia: Jewish Publication Society of America, 1913).

Rotenstreich, N., *Jewish Philosophy in Modern Times* (New York: Holt, Rinehart & Winston, 1968).

Rudavsky, David, *Emancipation and Adjustment* (New York: Diplomatic Press, 1967).

Simon, M., *Moses Mendelssohn: His Life and His Times* (London: Jewish Religious Educational Publications, 1953).

Walter, H., *Moses Mendelssohn: Critic and Philosopher* (New York: Bloch Publishing Co., 1930).

In addition, since 1955 the Leo Baeck Institute, founded by the Council of Jews from Germany, has been publishing a *Year Book* containing approximately twenty articles annually on various topics concerning the rise and development of German Jewry. Considerable attention has always been paid to Haskalah, Enlightenment, Reform, and Mendelssohn. See *Publications of the Leo Baeck Institute*, 1955– (London: Secker & Warburg).

Chapter 3: East European Jewry in Crisis: The Threat of the Modern Age

For nearly three decades the Yiddish Research Institute in New York (YIVO) has been publishing the *YIVO Annual of Jewish Social Science* in English, a series which provides a vast amount of material dealing with various aspects of East European Jewish life.

Abramovitch, Hirsch, "Rural Jewish Occupations in Lithuania," *YIVO Annual of Jewish Social Science,* vols. II and III, New York, 1947–1948.

Ain, Abraham, "Swislocz, Portrait of a Jewish Community in Eastern Europe," *YIVO Annual of Social Science,* vol. IV, New York, 1949.

Baron, S. W., *The Russian Jew Under Tsars and Soviets* (New York: Macmillan, 1964).

————, *A Social and Religious History of the Jews,* three vols. (New York: Columbia University Press, 1937).

Bram, Joseph, "The Social Identity of the Jews," *Transactions of the New York Academy of Sciences,* series II, vol. VI, 1944.

Cohen, Israel, *Jewish Life in Modern Times* (London: Methuen & Co., 1929).

Davidowicz, Lucy S., ed. *The Golden Tradition: Jewish Life and Thought in Eastern Europe, a Historical Introduction,* paperback (Boston: Beacon Press, 1968). The best source material available in English, along with an excellent essay.

Dubnow, Semen M., *History of the Jews in Russia and Poland* (Philadelphia: Jewish Publication Society of America, 1916–1920).

Elbogen, Isaac, *A Century of Jewish Life, 1840–1940* (Philadelphia: Jewish Publication Society of America, 1944).

Epstein, Louis M., *Sex Laws and Customs in Judaism* (New York: Bloch Publishing Co., 1948).

Feldman, W. M., *The Jewish Child* (London: Bailliere, Tindall and Cox, 1917).

Frumkin and others, eds., *Russian Jewry, 1860–1917* (New York: Thomas Yoseloff, 1966).

Goldin, H. E., *The Jewish Woman and Her Home* (New York: Jewish Culture Publishing Co., 1941).

Herzl, Theodor, *The Diaries*. Edited and translated by Lowenthal. (New York: Dial Press, 1956.)

Heschel, Abraham Joshua, *The Earth Is the Lord's: The Inner World of the Jew in East Europe* (New York: H. Schuman, 1950).

Howe, Irving and Eliezer Greenberg, eds., "Introduction," *A Treasury of Yiddish Stories* (New York: Schocken Books, 1973). Along with the Davidowicz essay, the most intelligent writing for the general public, in seventy pages.

Jiggets, J. Ida, *Religion, Diet and Health of Jews*, two vols. (New York: Bloch Publishing Co., 1949).

Lampert, E., *Sons Against Fathers: Studies in Russian Radicalism and Revolution* (London: Methuen & Co., 1965).

Landes, Ruth, and Mark Zborowski, "Hypotheses Concerning the Eastern European Jewish Family," *Psychiatry*, vol. XIII, 1950.

Levitats, Isaac, *The Jewish Community in Russia, 1772–1844* (New York: Columbia University Press, 1943).

Pinson, Koppel S., *Essays on Anti-Semitism*, new edition, revised (New York: New York Jewish Social Studies, 1942).

Philipson, David, *Old European Jewries* (Philadelphia: Jewish Publication Society of America, 1894).

Roskies, Diane K. and David G. Roskies, *The Shtetl Book* (New York: KTAV Publishing Co., 1975).

Weinryb, B. D., "East European Jewry Since the Partitions of Poland," in Finkelstein, ed., *The Jews: Their History, Culture, and Religion*, vol. I, op. cit.

Zborowski, Mark and Elizabeth Herzog, *Life Is with People: The Culture of the Shtetl* (New York: Schocken Books, 1962). A very popular and readable picture of *shtetl* life.

Zelkovitch, J., "A Picture of Communal Life of a Jewish Town in Poland in the Second Half of the Nineteenth Century," *YIVO Annual of Jewish Social Science*, vol. VI, New York, 1951.

Abramowitz and the Rise of Yiddish Literature
(Mendele Mocher Sforim)

Liptzin, Sol, *A History of Yiddish Literature* (New York: Jonathan David, 1972). The most thorough historical survey in English.

———, *The Flowering of Yiddish Literature* (New York: Thomas Yoseloff, 1963). Focuses more on the personalities. Good introduction to Mendele.

Mark, Judel, "Yiddish Literature," in Louis Finkelstein, *The Jews: Their History, Culture and Religion*, vol. II, op. cit.

Madison, Charles, *Yiddish Literature: Its Scope and Major Writers* (New York: Schocken Books, 1971). A thorough history, available in paperback.

Miron, Dan, *A Traveler Disguised: A Study in the Rise of Modern Yiddish Fiction in the Nineteenth Century* (New York: Schocken Books, 1973). An excellent introduction to *Haskalah* in the East and to the works of Mendele. Miron covers new ground for the English reader.

Chapter 4: Sholom Aleichem's Tevye Stories: The Crisis of Family Life

Sholom Aleichem (Sholom Rabinowitz) has been much translated in the past fifteen years, since the enormous success of *Fiddler on the Roof*. The following works are available in English:

The Great Fair: Scenes from My Childhood, Tamara Kahana, tr. (New York: Noonday Press, 1958). Sholom Aleichem's autobiography.

Adventures of Mottel, The Cantor's Son, Tamara Kahana, tr. (New York: Collier Books, 1961).

The Tevye Stories and Others, Julius and Frances Butwin, trs. (New York: Pocketbooks, Inc., 1965).

Some Laughter, Some Tears, Curt Leviant, tr. (New York: G. P. Putnam's Sons, 1968).

Old Country Tales, Curt Leviant, tr. (New York: G. P. Putnam's Sons, 1966).

Stories and Satires, Curt Leviant, tr. (New York: Thomas Yoseloff, 1959).

The Adventures of Menahem-Mendel, Tamara Kahana, tr. (New York: G. P. Putnam's Sons, 1969).

Tevye's Daughters, Frances Butwin, tr. (New York: Crown Publishers, 1949).

The Old Country, Julius and Frances Butwin, trs. (New York: Crown Publishers, 1946).

Wandering Star, Frances Butwin, tr. (New York: Crown Publishers, 1952).

There is a generous selection in Howe and Greenberg, eds., *A Treasury of Yiddish Stories*, op. cit.

A complete list of all works by Sholom Aleichem in both English and in Yiddish can be found in "Sholom Aleichem in English: The Most Accessible Translations," David Neal Miller, in *Yiddish: A Quarterly Journal*, vol. II, Queens College, New York, 1977.

Biography and Criticism

Butwin, Frances and Joseph Butwin, *Sholom Aleichem* (Boston: G. K. Hall & Co., 1977). This Twayne World Author Series volume is a good general introduction to the life and times.

Gittleman, Sol, *Sholom Aleichem: An Introduction* (The Hague: Mouton & Co., 1974).

Samuel, Maurice, *The World of Sholom Aleichem* (New York: Alfred A. Knopf, 1943).

Waife-Goldberg, Marie, *My Father, Sholom Aleichem* (New York: Simon & Shuster, 1968). A very personal memoir, reveals that there was a great deal of his characters in the man himself.

Wisse, Ruth R. *The Schlemiel as Modern Hero* (Chicago: University of Chicago Press, 1972). Goes back to the Yiddish traditions of American fiction.

Chapter 5: A Sociology of Mishpoche Stereotypes

The very best collections of Yiddish literature in English have come from the editing of Irving Howe and Eliezer Greenberg. The most comprehensive of their anthologies is *A Treasury of Yiddish Stories*, op. cit., which contains more than fifty stories representative of the writings of Mendele, Sholom Aleichem, Peretz, Pinski, Asch, Reisen, Schneour, both Singers, and others. Howe & Greenberg have also edited and translated *A Treasury of Yiddish Poetry* (New York: Schocken Books, 1974), *Selected Stories of I. L. Peretz* (New York: Schocken Books, 1974), and *Ashes Out of Hope: Fiction by Soviet-Yiddish Writers* (New York: Schocken Books, 1977). Other recommended translations of collections and individual authors are as follows:

Asch, Sholem, *Three Cities*, Edwin and Willa Muir, trs. (New York: G. P. Putnam's Sons, 1943).

———, *Mottke the Thief*, Edwin and Willa Muir, trs. (New York: G. P. Putnam's Sons, 1917).

Bellow, Saul, ed., *Great Jewish Short Stories* (New York: Dell, 1966). Contains Yiddish, Hebrew, and American stories, most impressive of which is Bellow's own translation of I. B. Singer's "Gimpel the Fool."

Leftwich, Joseph, *An Anthology of Modern Yiddish Literature* (The Hague: Mouton, 1974). An excellent collection of stories, plays, essays, and poetry.

Mendele, *The Nag*, Moshe Spiegel, tr. (New York: Thomas Yoseloff, 1958).

————, The Parasite, Gerald Stillman, tr. (New York: Thomas Yoseloff, 1958).

————, The Travels of Benjamin the Third, Moshe Spiegel, tr. (New York: Schocken Books, 1958).

Singer, I. B., Gimpel the Fool (New York: Farrar, Straus & Giroux, 1951).

————, The Spinoza of Market Place (New York: Farrar, Straus & Giroux, 1951).

————, Satan in Goray (New York: Farrar, Straus & Giroux, 1955).

————, The Magician of Lublin (New York: Farrar, Straus & Giroux, 1960).

————, My Father's Court (New York: Farrar, Straus & Giroux, 1966).

————, Mazel and Schlimazel (New York: Farrar, Straus & Giroux, 1967).

————, Short Friday (New York: Farrar, Straus & Giroux, 1966).

————, A Friend of Kafka (New York: Farrar, Straus & Giroux, 1972).

Singer, I. J., The Brothers Ashkenazi (New York: Alfred A. Knopf, 1933).

————, Yoshe Kalb (New York: Liveright, 1933; new ed. Vanguard Press, 1976).

————, The Family Carnovsky (New York: Vanguard Press, 1969).

Two collections that deserve special attention are:

Yenne Velt: The Great Works of Jewish Fantasy & Occult, two vols., Joachim Neugroschel, ed. (New York: Stonehill Publishing Co., 1976). This is an extraordinary collection of material ranging from Kabbalah to the modern period.

Epic and Folk Plays of the Yiddish Theatre, David S. Lifson, ed. & tr. (Rutherford, N.J.: Fairleigh Dickinson University Press, 1975). The first modern collection of Yiddish plays, excluding those of Ansky's The Dybbuk.

Chapter 6: Yiddishkeit on Two Continents

The Immigrant Experience

Irving Howe's masterful World of Our Fathers (New York: Harcourt Brace Jovanovich, 1976), has made much more bibliography unnecessary. This huge volume chronicles the entire experience of the Jew from the Old World to the New World and concentrates on life on the Lower East Side of New York.

A SELECTIVE REFERENCE BIBLIOGRAPHY IN ENGLISH

The following are a few specialized works of interest on the subject of the immigrant Jew:

Davidowicz, Lucy S., "Transformations: The American Catalyst," in *The Jewish Presence* (New York: Holt, Rinehart & Winston, 1977). An evocative essay on the transition of the Jew into American society.

Hapgood, Hutchins, *The Spirit of the Ghetto: Studies of the Jewish Quarter of New York* (New York: Schocken Books, 1966). Written in the early years of the century by a New York reporter, this is a remarkable eyewitness account.

Handlin, Oscar, *The Uprooted* (Boston: Beacon Press, 1951). The trials of leaving the familiar world for the uncertainties of America.

Hubmann, Franz, *The Jewish Family Album; The Life of a People in Photographs* (Boston: Little, Brown, 1975). The most comprehensive pictorial history of the various centers of Jewish life during the last hundred years.

Kessner, Thomas, *The Golden Door: Italian and Jewish Immigrant Mobility in New York City, 1880–1915* (New York: Oxford University Press, 1977). The Jew and Italian living together and rising from poverty.

Metzker, Isaac, ed., with introduction, *A Bintel Brief. A Collection of Letters from the Jewish Daily Forward* (New York: Ballantine Books, 1971). Remarkable letters to editor Abraham Cahan of the *Forward*, filled with the texture of Jewish life on the Lower East Side of New York.

Sandrow, Nahma, *Vagabond Stars: A World History of Yiddish Theatre* (New York: Harper & Row, 1977). The chapters on theatre in America are excellent.

Schoener, Allon, ed., *Portal to America: The Lower East Side, 1870–1925* (New York: Holt, Rinehart & Winston, 1967). The source of most of the pictures found in other collections. In addition, contemporary newspaper articles written by reporters from the *New York Tribune, World,* and *Times,* describing life in New York's ghetto around the turn of the century.

The German Jew and the Rise of Hitler: The Holocaust
Again, the publications of the Leo Baeck Institute deal exclusively and exhaustively with the fate of German Jewry.

Davidowicz, Lucy, *The War Against the Jews, 1933–1945* (New York: Holt, Rinehart, & Winston, 1975).

Glatstein, Knox, and Margoshes, eds., *A Reader of Holocaust Literature* (Philadelphia: Jewish Publication Society of America, 1968).

Friedlander, A., ed., *Out of the Whirlwind: A Reader of Holocaust Literature* (New York: Union of American Jewish Congregations, 1968).

Gay, Peter, *Freud, the Germans and the Jews* (New York: Oxford University Press, 1968). A series of provocative essays chronicling the dilemma and tragedy of German Jewry.

Hilberg, Raul, *The Destruction of European Jewry* (Chicago: Quadrangle Books, 1961). Enormous documentation.

Mosse, George, *The Germans and the Jews* (New York: Grosset & Dunlap, 1970).

———, *The Crisis of German Ideology; Intellectual Origins of the Third Reich* (New York: Grosset & Dunlap, 1964).

Poliakov, Leon, *Harvest of Hate: The Nazi Program for the Destruction of the Jews of Europe* (Syracuse: University of Syracuse Press, 1954).

Reitlinger, Gerald, *The Final Solution*, 2nd edition (New York: Thomas Yoseloff, 1968).

Tartakower, A., "The Decline of European Jewry, 1933–1953," in Louis Finkelstein, ed., *The Jews: Their History, Culture and Religion*, 3rd ed., vol. I, op. cit.

Jews and the Soviet Union

A special word about Lawrence Langer, *The Holocaust and the Literary Imagination* (New Haven: Yale University Press, 1975). The first attempt to come to grips with the imaginative literature that grew out of the experience of the destruction of European Jewry. A remarkable achievement.

The two most useful collections of Yiddish literature written in the Soviet Union are:

Howe and Greenberg, *Ashes Out of Hope*, op. cit. An excellent introduction and five elegantly translated short stories of four Yiddish writers who died during the Stalinist purges.

Leftwich, Joseph, *An Anthology of Modern Yiddish Literature*. A more comprehensive anthology, includes a good foreword and useful biographical material on Polish and Russian Yiddishists. Short stories, essays, and poetry (Atlantic Highlands, N.J.: Humanities Press, 1974).

Chapter 7: From Shtetl to Suburbia
The Sociology of Jewish American Life.

The literature is enormous and growing. What follows is no more than a useful selection:

Fuchs, Lawrence, *The Political Behavior of American Jews* (New York: The Free Press, 1956).

Gans, Herbert, "Progress of a Suburban Jewish Community," *Commentary*, February 1957.

Gay, Ruth, *The Jews in America* (New York: Basic Books, 1965).

Gelber, S. M., "Does the Jewish Past Have a Jewish Future?" in *Essays on Jewish Life and Thought,* edited by Joseph L. Blau (New York: Columbia University Press, 1959).

Glazer, Nathan, "Social Characteristics of American Jews," *American Jewish Year Book*, 1955.

Gordon, A. I., *Jews in Suburbia* (Boston: Beacon Press, 1959).

Lauter, Paul, "Reflections of a Jewish Activist," *Conservative Judaism*, 1965.

Lewin, Kurt, "Self-Hate Among Jews," in *Resolving Social Conflicts*, G. W. Lewin, ed. (New York: Harper & Row, 1948).

Neusner, Jacob, "The New Orthodox Left," in *Conservative Judaism*, Fall 1965.

Roche, John P., *The Quest for the Dream* (New York: Macmillan, 1963).

Sklar, Marshall, ed., *The Jews: Social Patterns of an American Group* (New York: The Free Press, 1958). A very useful collection of essays on Jewish immigration, assimilation, demography, self-study.

Contemporary Jewish Literature in America

An immense body of secondary literature and literary criticism on individual Jewish-American writers has developed, particularly since Bellow's winning of the Nobel Prize for literature. Indeed, anthologies of criticism *about* Malamud, Bellow, Roth and others have already appeared. There are two notable collections of literature, however, that do require mention:

Chapman, Abraham, ed., *Jewish-American Literature: An Anthology,* a Mentor Book (New York: New American Library, 1974). A collection of fiction, poetry, autobiography, memoir and criticism dealing with "the cultural chemistry" of Jewish writing in America. A very useful book.

Howe, Irving, ed., *Jewish-American Stories,* with an Introduction (New York: New American Library, 1977). Contains an excellent collection of the best fiction dealing with the theme of the Jew in America, along with an exceptionally perceptive essay by Howe.

Notes

1. In the languages of the Gypsies and the Armenians one encounters the same linguistic separation of "us" from "them." In Romany-Gypsie, the word for anyone not a Gypsy is "gaje"; in Armenian, it is "oddah." In Hebrew and Yiddish, it is "goy." Each of these terms carries with it associations of stupidity, brutality, and the threat to the existence of the minority describing the "outsider."

Chapter 1

1. "Early commentators identified the word *Sepharad*, which appears in *Obadiah* 9:20, with the country of Spain. As a result, the Jews of the Iberian Peninsula and their descendants came to be known as *Sephardim*, as distinct from the Jews of the Franco-German tradition, who are known as *Ashkenazim* (*Ashkenaz* in *Genesis* 10:3 having been identified with Germany). After the expulsion of the Jews from Spain in 1492 the word *Sephardi* was given wider connotation as the Jews from Spain imposed their culture and traditions upon the Jewish communities of North Africa and the Middle East." *The Encyclopedia of the Jewish Religion*, Werblowsky & Wigoder, eds. (New York: Holt, Rinehart & Winston, 1965), 347–48.

2. Technically, Jews had been banished from entire countries of the West: in 1290 from England; in 1306 from France; and in 1492 from Spain. But some court Jews were no doubt permitted to stay on.

3. The most impressive memoir in Yiddish produced in the early Yiddish period was that of Gluckel of Hameln (1645–1724), one of the first emancipated women of European Jewry.

4. *Das Deutsche Gaunertum in seiner social-politischen, literarischen und linguistischen Ausbildung zu seinem heutigen Bestande* (Leipzig, 1858–64), vier Bände.

Chapter 2

1. In Kabbalistic literature, the union of God is described in strictly masculine and feminine terms. *Tiferet* and *Shechinah* must be joined in union if God is to appear.

2. *History of the Jews* (Philadelphia: Jewish Publication Soc., 1895), vol. 5, 335.

3. The Lubavitcher Hassidim have created the concept of the "Mitzvot Mobile," a portable vehicle found in most of America's big cities, staffed by street-hawking followers who are apt to walk up to a prospective customer and confront him with the question: "Are you a Jew?" An affirmative answer is followed by a gentle but persuasive sales pitch on the Lubavitcher movement.

4. This accounts for the attractive nature of Germanized Jewish

NOTES

names: Blumenthal (Valley of Flowers); Rosenberg (Rose Mountain);
Bernstein (Amber); Schoenberg (Beautiful Mountain), etc. The Jews
selected aesthetically lovely names. However, some orthodox Jews refused the order to take a non-Hebrew name, and the authorities somewhat maliciously gave them less attractive ones: ergo, Schlanger
(snake), Goldwasser (urine).

Chapter 3
1. The Skvira Hassidim have kept alive the name of their community
even in America. They are the inhabitants of the incorporated village
of New Square, near Muncie, New York.
2. The village beggar enjoyed some status, however. A Kabbalistic-
Hassidic legend concerns the *lamed vavs*, the thirty-six Jewish saints
whom God has placed on earth to justify the world's existence. They
are hidden, modest, and sometimes beggars. As a result, taking advantage of the fact that they might be potential *lamed-vavs*, Jewish
beggars often became quite aggressive.
3. According to Maimonides, the pious Jew has 613 commandments
to fulfill. However, the Jewish woman is required to honor merely
three: the lighting of the *Shabbes* candles, the baking of *Shabbes*
bread, and the maintenance of ritual purity, over her home and herself.
4. It was considered bad luck to have only daughters. Only a son
could say the *Kaddish* prayer for his dead parents.
5. *Shlemihl* etymologically has not been fully explained; *shlimmazel*
comes from the German *schlimm*, bad; and the Hebrew *mazel*, luck.

Chapter 4
1. Quoted in the *New York Times Book Review*, July 10, 1977, p. 3.
2. In English, *Some Laughter, Some Tears*, translated by Curt Leviant,
New York, G. P. Putnam's Sons, 1968, 128. In Yiddish the story may be
found in *Ale Verke*, Folksfund edition, vol. VIII, *Mayses far yidishe
kinder*, pp. 7–32.
3. He did return for a brief and triumphant lecture and reading tour
shortly before the outbreak of hostilities.
4. *The World of Sholom Aleichem*: New York, Schocken, 1965, p. 330.
5. In *The Tevye Stories*, trans. Butwin (New York: Pocket Books Inc.,
1965), pp. 126–42; in Yiddish, Vol. V of the *Ale Verke*, Folksfund Edition, pp. 13–40.
6. The authors of the popular musical adaptation of the Tevye
stories, called *Fiddler on the Roof*, had a remarkable grasp of the
marital facts of life in the *shtetl*. Golde cannot respond to the question
in the song "Do You Love Me?" Love was not usually a prerequisite
for the traditional *shtetl* marriage.
7. *The Tevye Stories*, pp. 1–15; Vol. V of the *Ale Verke*, pp. 41–63.
8. Menachem Mendel is the figure in an epistolary novel devoted

solely to his woes, *The Adventures of Menachem Mendel,* translated by Tamara Kahana (New York: G. P. Putnam's Sons, 1969). In Yiddish, Vol. X of the Folksfund edition of *Ale Verke.*

9. In *The Tevye Stories,* pp. 16–32; *Ale Verke,* Vol. V, pp. 67–91.

10. In *The Tevye Stories,* pp. 41–52; also in *A Treasury of Yiddish Stories,* ed. Howe & Greenberg (New York: Schocken, 1973), pp. 168–173; in *Ale Verke,* Vol. V, pp. 95–118.

11. In *Tevye Stories,* pp. 61–75; in *Ale Verke,* Vol. V, pp. 121–40.

12. In *The Tevye Stories,* pp. 76–89; in *Ale Verke,* Vol. V, pp. 143–163.

13. In *Tevye Stories,* pp. 91–110; in *Ale Verke,* Vol. V, pp. 167–95.

Chapter 5

1. New York: Random House, 1969.

2. The image of the bad *nogid* is consistent throughout Sholom Aleichem's works. See "The Yom Kippur Scandal" and "The Passover Expropriation."

3. It was Saul Bellow's translation of this story which helped create a reading public for Singer in English.

Chapter 6

1. Hitler did permit Helene Meyer, the medalist fencer living in America, a half-Jewess, to join the German team, partly because she was a blond-haired, blue-eyed beauty.

2. See the remarkable memoir by Jörg von Uthmann, personal secretary to the first German ambassador to Israel, *Doppelgänger, du bleicher Geselle* (Stuttgart: Seewald, 1976).

3. Ironically, German soldiers in World War I who crossed into Poland wrote back astonished letters to their parents, saying that "we have met some strange people who speak our Nibelungen German!"

4. A story by Lamed Shapiro, "White Challah," deals with this period.

5. The anthology edited by Irving Howe and Eliezer Greenberg, *Ashes Out of Hope* (New York: Schocken Books, 1977), provides selections from the works of David Bergelson, Moshe Kulbak, and Der Nister in excellent translations.

6. Stephen Birmingham's *Our Crowd* (paperback ed., New York: Pocket Books, 1977) remains a good, general source book on New York's German Jews.

7. Irving Howe's masterful *World of Our Fathers* (New York: Harcourt Brace Jovanovich, 1976), gives the most vivid picture of these early years of life in the Jewish ghetto.

8. The image of the Jewish underworld never caught the imagination of America, primarily because Italians and Irish were singled out, particularly in the motion picture, as the overlords of crime. Ironically, it was Lower East Side Jews who went to Hollywood and who encouraged this. Sam Goldwyn, Louis B. Mayer, Adolph Zukor, Harry Cohn,

and the Warner Brothers insisted that Cagney and Edward G. Robinson die in the arms of a priest—inevitably Pat O'Brien. It would have been historically just as accurate if a Jewish gunman had died in the arms of a rabbi.

9. The Yiddish is *a stimme vie a feygel.* The use of *feygel* implies that Van Sickel is effeminate.

Chapter 7

1. This is the title of a book edited by Madison Grant and Charles S. Davison, written in 1930. A few quotes follow: "Irish immigrants had neither the temperament nor the training to make a success of popular government. . . . That the Mediterranean peoples are morally below the races of northern Europe is as certain as any social act. . . . In ignorance and illiteracy, in coarseness and low standards of cleanliness, a large part of the Slavic world remains at the level of our English forefathers in the days of Henry VIII."

2. *World of Our Fathers,* 412.

3. Jewish faculty members, particularly in English departments, also faced similar discrimination. Ironically, this discrimination had become institutionalized and lionized in the critical methodology known as the New Criticism, a method which excludes all "extrinsic" materials, i.e., sociology, psychology, environment, heritage, etc., in analysis of the work of literature, in favor of an "intrinsic" method of close textual reading of the work. The founding fathers of this idea were Ezra Pound and T. S. Eliot, who turned to Henry James as a model in fiction. All three shared a hatred of a mongrelized America filled with immigrants; ethnic literature would have filled them with contempt. On the other hand, Jewish-American English scholars looked to the New Criticism as an aid in escaping from the ghetto, as a means of erasing their background through "pure" criticism. It was the generation of Jewish-Americans who finally broke through the barriers of discrimination who were the greatest advocates of the new critical style. It was the academic counterpart to cultural assimilation, and the loss of Jewish identity.

4. American Conservative Judaism was a response to the apparent end of orthodox Judaism and the threat of the rising Reform Movement.

5. Ironically, it was a kind of throwback ethnic from Brockton, Massachusetts, Rocky Marciano, who in the fifties interrupted black dominance in the heavyweight division.

6. See Sol Liptzin, *Germany's Stepchildren* (Philadelphia: Jewish Publication Society of America, 1944).

7. Chicago: University of Chicago Press, 1971.

8. Another remarkable irony of this renaissance was the fate of I. B. Singer, one of the few surviving Yiddish writers, who was "rediscovered" at the same time and whom Bellow had translated into English.

It was in the English language that Singer finally found an audience far greater than he ever enjoyed in his original Yiddish. Yet he writes only in Yiddish, and his works are then translated into English. Henry Roth as well was only read thirty years after his novel was written.

9. Roth, Malamud, and Bellow are three of twenty-five writers included in Irving Howe's anthology of *Jewish-American Stories* (New York: New American Library, a Mentor Book, 1977). The first story in the collection is one by Sholom Aleichem.

10. In *Goodbye, Columbus* (New York: Modern Library, 1966).

11. In *The Magic Barrel* (New York: Farrar, Straus & Giroux, 1958).

12. Ibid.

13. Ibid.

14. New York: Farrar, Straus & Giroux, 1966.

15. New York: Farrar, Straus & Giroux, 1957.

16. Beiliss was the last Jew accused by the Czarist government of having killed a Gentile child and used the blood for Passover Matzohs. This famous 1911 case caused an uproar all over Europe.

17. "The First Seven Years," "The Angel Levine," "The Mourners," and "The Loan" are all in *The Magic Barrel,* op. cit.

18. In Malamud's "Angel Levine" the theme of the dead son stricken down early in life heightens the tragedy for the Jewish parent, as it does here.

19. New York: Viking Press, 1970.

20. New York: Farrar, Straus & Giroux, 1961.

21. New York: Random House, 1967.

22. New York: Vanguard Press, 1959.

23. Bellow was participating in a groundswell of American public opinion which at the time viewed New York as a kind of magnet for everything that was wrong with this country. The motion picture industry, always sensitive to public opinion, capitalized with a number of "hate New York" films: *Death Wish; The Taking of Pelham One, Two, Three; Law and Disorder;* and *The Out-of-Towners* were just a few. New York suggested corruption, filth, anarchy. It is not surprising that New York's fiscal difficulties were met with indifference by the rest of the country.

Glossary

A note on spelling Yiddish words in English. There is no official set of rules to follow in transliterating Yiddish forms into English. I generally have attempted to avoid Germanisms by using "sh" instead of "sch" whenever possible, but there is no consistent spelling which makes all Yiddishists happy. The variations on individual words are apparently endless. See, for instance, *Hassidism, Hasidism, Chassidism, Chasidism;* even the name of the famous Yiddish writer appears as Sholem Aleichem, Sholom Aleychem, Shalom Aleichem, and other spellings. Therefore I have simply aimed at consistency.

Ashkenaz: Hebrew name for Germany.

Ashkenazi, pl. *Ashkenazim:* originally, Jews from Germany; later, all East European Jews; also, identifiable as any Yiddish-speaking Jew.

Baal Shem Tov: "Master of the Good Name" (the *Besht,* in abbreviated form), Israel Ben Elizer, c. 1700–1760, the founder of Hassidism.

Bar Mitzvah: the religious ceremony at which the thirteen-year-old Jewish male becomes a member of the community.

Bobe-mayse: a fantastic tale; from the Hebrew word for story (*mayse*), and confusion between the Italian *Bovo* and the Yiddish for grandmother, *bobe,* which led to the meaning "a tale told by a grandmother."

Bund: a socialist organization of Jewish workers.

Chutzpah: nerve, effrontery.

Converso: Spanish, a term applied to apparent Jewish converts to Christianity who still maintained a cryptic Jewish identity.

Diaspora: Greek, the Jewish exile from Palestine after the defeat by the Romans in 70 A. D.

Gaje: Romany-Gypsie, an outsider, a non-Gypsy, an alien.

Galizianer: a Jew from Galicia in Poland; by extension, any Polish Jew.

Ganef: exists in Hebrew, Yiddish, and German, and means thief; also found in American slang. A word from the Yiddish underworld.

Gaon: in Hebrew, an outstanding scholar. A term used for centuries, applied particularly in connection with Elijah Ben Solomon Zalman of Vilna (1720–1797), the orthodox opponent of Hassidism, known as the Vilna Gaon.

Gaunersprache: German, the language of the underworld, in the late Middle Ages synonymous with Yiddish.

Goy, pl. *Goyim:* literally, in Hebrew, people of the nation. In Yiddish, any non-Jew, or Gentile.

Goyish: Actions considered un-Jewish.

Haskalah: Hebrew, the Enlightenment, the intellectual movement which spread from Germany in the eighteenth century, encouraging modernization and secularization of Jewish life.

Hassid, pl. *Hassidim:* Hebrew, the pious people. A term used in the Middle Ages, it became associated with the followers of the movement begun by the Baal Shem Tov in the eighteenth century.

Hassidism: a religious revolution which swept through East European Jewry in the eighteenth century; advocated a joyous and simple union with God. The founder was Israel Ben Elizer, the Baal Shem Tov.

Hofjuden: court Jews in Germany.

Ivri-Teutsch: during the emergence of Yiddish from German, a name given by the Germans to describe either the German spoken by the Jews, or a text translated from Hebrew into German using Hebrew letters.

Judezmo: see *Ladino*

Jüdisch: German, as spoken by Jews in the Rhineland during the period of language formation of Yiddish.

Judenteutsch: similarly, in German, the language spoken by the Jewish population of the Rhineland during the Middle Ages.

Kabbalah: the sum total of the writings on Jewish mysticism.

Kiddush Hashem: Hebrew, "Sanctification of the Name," or martyrdom. The title of a story by Sholem Asch.

Kinder: children

Koved: honor, respect

Laaz: Franco-German, primarily a dialect of Old French, with some Germanic intrusion, and spoken in France at the time of Rashi in the tenth and eleventh centuries.

Ladino: Spanish, or *Judezmo,* Judaeo-Spanish, the language of the Spanish Jews, and later of the Levantine Jews in Turkey. The language of the *Sephardim.*

Lamed vav: Hebrew, for thirty-six. The legend of the thirty-six just human beings for whom God maintains the existence of Mankind. A legend derived from Talmudic times but which became popular in Eastern Europe; usually a humble, poor *shlemihl.* In fiction, Bontsha and Gimpel would be considered *lamed vav.*

Litvak: a Jew from Lithuania; by extension, eventually any Jew from Russia, as opposed to a Galizianer, a Jew from Poland.

Loshen ha-kodesh: Hebrew, the Holy Tongue, i.e., the Hebrew language, reserved from religious and spiritual use.

Luftmensh: literally, a man of air, a *shtetl* Jew without a steady income or a means of earning a living.

Mama-loshen: "the mother's tongue," Yiddish.

Marrano: Spanish, "swine" or "pig": a term applied to converted Jews who in spite of outward appearance continued to practice Judaism during the Spanish Middle Ages and into the period of the Inquisition.

Matzoh: unleavened bread eaten during Passover.

Maskil, plural, *Maskilim:* Hebrew, an enlightened individual, a follower of the Haskalah, a modern Jew.

Mazel: luck.

Mazeltov!: Good luck!

Mezuzah: Hebrew, an object attached to the doorposts of Jewish homes, containing a portion of the Pentateuch.

Mishpoche: universal Jewish word for "family"; any relative; any Jew.

Mitnagged, pl. *Mitnaggedim:* Hebrew, "opponent"; any enemy of Hassidism.

Mitzvah: command; act of piety which one Jew performs for another; a good deed.

Moses Ben Maimon: Hebrew name of Maimonides, also called the *Rambam* (1135–1204), the greatest figure of medieval Spanish Jewry, a codifier, philosopher, and scholar.

Naches: pleasure, joy, gratification: "what one should get from children."

Nogid, pl. *Negidim:* the rich Jew of the *shtetl.*

Oddah: Armenian, "the outsider," any non-Armenian.

Parnosseh: a living, occupation; how a Jew earns a livelihood.

Pilpul: Hebrew, for pepper. The scholastic, dialectical interpretation of biblical or Talmudic texts indulged in by Yeshiva students. Often degenerated into narrow pedantry.

Prost: simple, ordinary.

Proste yidn: common, ordinary Jews of the *shtetl.*

Rabbiner: a state-appointed rabbi in Czarist Russia, very unpopular in the *shtetl.*

Rashi: abbreviated name of Rabbi Solomon Ben Isaac of Troyes (1040–1105), great French Talmudic and biblical scholar.

Reb: equivalent of Mister, a title of respect. It is important for Tevye that he become "Reb Tevye."

Rosh Hashonah: the Jewish New Year.

Schutzjuden: protected Jews in a German principality.

Seyfer, pl. *Sforim:* Hebrew, for "book," as in Mendele Mochir Sforim, "Mendele the Seller of Books," pseudonym of Sholom Abramovitch.

Sepharad: Hebrew name for Spain.

Sephardi, pl. *Sephardim:* Spanish Jews.

Shabbes: the Sabbath.

Shabbes Goy: the Christian who will do work for a Jew on the Sabbath which the Jew is forbidden to perform.

Shadchan: the matchmaker, the marriage broker.

Shaygitz: a non-Jewish young man.

Shayne yidn: upper-class Jews.

Sheytl: a wig worn by orthodox Jewish women.

Shiksa: a non-Jewish young woman.

Shlemihl: the submissive fool of the *shtetl;* the ultimate Jewish loser, gullible, innocent, weak, the eternal victim.

Shlimmazel: the *shtetl* inhabitant plagued by bad luck and worse fortune. From the Hebrew "mazel" (luck) and the German "schlimm" (bad).

Shnorrer: the *shtetl* beggar.

Sholom Aleichem: "Peace be unto you."

Shoychet: the ritual slaughterer.

Shtetl: small town or village in Eastern Europe, with a major Jewish population.

Shvartse: a black maid or cleaning woman.

Talmud: the basic body of Jewish law.

Torah: Jewish teachings; also, the five books of Moses; the entire body of Jewish learning.

Tzaddik, pl. *Tzaddikim:* Hassidic leader or wise man.

Tzurus: troubles.

Yeshiva: a Jewish academy of learning.

Yid, pl. *Yidn:* when Jews refer to themselves; also, a slang term used by Gentiles in a negative sense.

Yiddish: Jewish; the Jewish language, the vernacular language of the Jews.

Yiddishkeit: Jewishness, the Jewish way of life, Jewish life in Eastern Europe.

Yichus: status in the community, in the *shtetl,* one's position in the social order.

Yom Kippur: the Day of Atonement, the holiest day in the Jewish year.

Zohar: the first of the great Kabbalistic writings, from the thirteenth century.

Index